D0927389

RIGHT TURN

HUTCHINSON RADIUS

RIGHT TURN

THE CONSERVATIVE REVOLUTION IN EDUCATION

Ken Jones

HUTCHINSON RADIUS

London Sydney Auckland Johannesburg

LC
93
G7
J66
1989

Hutchinson Radius
An imprint of Century Hutchinson Ltd
62–65 Chandos Place, London WC2N 4NW

Century Hutchinson Australia Pty Ltd
89–91 Albion Street, Surry Hills, New
South Wales 2010, Australia

Century Hutchinson New Zealand Limited
PO Box 40–086, Glenfield, Auckland 10,
New Zealand

Century Hutchinson South Africa (Pty) Ltd,
PO Box 337, Bergvlei, 2012 South Africa

First published by Hutchinson Radius 1989

© Ken Jones 1989

British Library Cataloguing in Publication Data

Jones, Ken, *1950–*
Right turn: the Conservative revelation in education.
1. Great Britain. Education. Policies of government
I. Title
379.41

ISBN 0 09 173217 4

ROBERT MANNING
STROZIER LIBRARY

MAR 28 1990

Tallahassee, Florida

Photoset in North Wales by
Derek Doyle & Associates, Mold, Clwyd
Printed and bound in Great Britain by
Mackays of Chatham

Contents

Preface

This book is partly a summary of the Conservative achievement in education. It is also an argument with it. In the course of that argument, it tries to define and explain the success of the Conservatives in education, as well as to criticise the nature of their project, and to dispute the likelihood of their lasting triumph.

These concerns occupy the first four chapters of the book. Chapter 1 outlines the stages of Conservative policy since the electoral defeats of 1974, and sets out the most prominent features of present policy. Chapters 2 and 3 distinguish the overlapping and sometimes competing strains within that policy. In doing so, these chapters make a distinction between what, for ease of exposition rather than strictness of designation, they term the Conservative 'right', and other tendencies which are given the label 'modernising'. Chapter 4 assesses the strengths, the problems and the weaknesses of the policy synthesis which the meeting of these various currents has created.

Throughout these chapters runs a persistent sub-theme, which contrasts the verve of the right's policy to the fragility and self-doubt which has overcome those who have been the historic defenders of the cause of educational reform. In Chapter 5, this issue becomes the explicit focus of the presentation. The chapter examines that mixture of occasional resistance and increasingly habitual accommodation with which the 'equal opportunity' tradition has responded to a rampant Conservatism. It notes, and argues against, the intellectual and political concessions that have been made. Out of that argument, it tries to develop a response of its own that is set out, first as discussion, then as manifesto, in the final chapter.

I described the book as an argument. This is true, I think, in a stronger sense than usually applies. The book does not aim only to present a case. For much of the time, it proceeds by encounter – literally by argument – with positions whose attractions it recognises and sometimes seeks to evoke, but whose claims it rejects. At a time when the ideas of the right are so ascendant in public debate, this can be a dangerous method of presentation: perhaps the evocation of opponents' ideas will prove more alluring than one's own. I don't think so, finally. But to write in this style – on what sometimes seems the brink of celebrating the success of ideas I am very far from sharing – is one way of recognising what too many, still, deny. In certain ways, Conservatism in education has made contact with popular discontents, and has been decisive in linking education to overall strategy. The power of its arguments has to be registered, or a strategy for its defeat will not develop.

As well as particular choices of style, there are also some issues of terminology and focus which need to be explained. For the most part, the book's concerns are contained within English, not 'British', boundaries. Scotland has not experienced the full blast of Tory radicalism in education. The Scottish teachers' union, the Educational Institute of Scotland, was much more effective than its counterparts in England and Wales in fighting off attacks on its negotiating rights. And the strike and demonstration it organised in late 1988, against what it called 'anglicisation' – the extension of the ideas of the Education Reform Act to Scotland – demonstrate very clearly that the analysis this book offers of Conservative success cannot justifiably be extended north of the border. The case of Wales is more difficult. Every aspect of Conservative education policy applies with equal force west of the Severn, and the impact of economic change since 1979 has been to accelerate the anglicisation of many areas of the country. Yet there are enough differences between the educational, and the political, climates of Wales and England, to make a simple inclusion of the Welsh dimension within the English hard to justify. In some ways, a specifically Welsh version of the 'national' curriculum, centred on the Welsh language, on Welsh literature written in English, and on Welsh history, is developing. The book does not focus on these differences, but it is aware of them. It uses 'English', not as a synonym for 'British', but as a term that relates to distinct, national features. 'British' is reserved for describing either an experience which is genuinely held in common, or for the British state.

There is also an issue of political terminology. In order to distinguish the mainstream of 'equal opportunity reform' from more radical tendencies, I frequently use the terms 'social democratic' or 'reform' to describe the first of these currents, and the unavoidably imprecise term 'the left' to signify the others. This usage, I need to stress, entails no suggestion that *only* the latter tendencies merit such a term being applied to them. Once again, it is a matter of convenient abbreviation, rather than of strict classification.

There is one final issue that concerns the limitations of this book. My experience of teaching has been in secondary schools; the main target of Conservative polemic and policy has likewise been secondary education. Out of these two factors is born the book's emphasis on this one particular sector. Post-16 developments have been more than adequately treated in other works, by Dan Finn, Phil Cohen, Caroline Benn and John Fairley. Changes in primary education still await such detailed, critical investigation – though I believe that the lines of inquiry that are begun here are relevant in such a project.

Finally, I owe much to those with whom I have discussed this book, or who have commented on it. They may recognise their ideas in parts of the book, however much they may disagree with others. I would especially like to thank Farhana Sheikh, Richard Hatcher, Hilda Kean, Paul Foley, Eddie Playfair, Bill Schwarz, Neil Belton and Mark Cohen. I am also indebted to the staff at the library of the National Union of Teachers, especially Janet Friedlander.

1

Outlines and histories

Conservative education policy, Janus-headed, fuses the archaic and the modern, mixes nostalgia with technology, evokes community and promotes entrepreneurialism. Its system of combining contrasts, linked polarities – and continuous tensions – is a complex one, that much of this book is devoted to following. Even at the outset, though, it is possible to make one plain assertion: the comforts that derive from seeing Conservative policy as an irrational spasm of reaction, that is by implication a mere interlude in the course of progress, must be forsaken.

So often, Conservative education policy is described as a regression: a backward step; a restoration of privilege; a return to selection. Indeed, it is very easy to think of the policy and its justifications in these ways. Nostalgia is one of their components, and restoration and a kind of re-established continuity are among the promises they make. But to notice these aspects alone is to gain only the most partial of understandings. In its centralizing form, the 1988 Education Reform Act may well (as critics like Brian Simon claim) reproduce features of the Conservative legislation of 1902. Likewise, the conceptions of curriculum content held by the Department of Education and Science (DES) and by many ministers reflect the influence of an academic and selective tradition. More important, though, than these echoes or repetitions is the novelty of Conservative policy. Even the most apparently archaic of its formulations serves a kind of contemporary purpose, and much of its programme has an explicit modernizing intent. Whether traditional or technological in their rhetoric, its various forms centre on at least one urgent common purpose: to eliminate the major tendencies that have dominated post-war education policy, and to replace them with a quite different order of priorities.

1

The first of these tendencies concerns the relationship between education and the economy. With increasing sureness, driven by the statements of the business lobby and given authority by passionate and well-documented academic studies, like those of Correlli Barnett, some Conservative politicians have identified the century-old weakness of English education: its remoteness from – or hostility to – industrial policy. Industrial training, they argue, has always been rudimentary; higher education has neglected the research needs of industry; schools have lacked interest in technology; and, perhaps most devastatingly of all, the English intelligentsia has developed a thoroughly anti-industrial ethos. Cultivating literary, historical or religious interests at the expense of a culture based around engineering and science, and prioritizing social integration above economic growth, it has helped create a disposition which, while favourable to costly projects of social reform, has displayed scorn, ignorance or fear of the necessities of technological development. In the schools, these interests have been reflected in the prestige and influence of particular subjects, in the selection of priorities within a subject area, and in a pervasive, non-competitive ethos.

It is one priority of the Conservative educational programme to change all this. Science and technology will become central to the national curriculum. New and well-funded schools will specialize in technical studies. The spirit of enterprise, the development of economic understanding, and of a 'motivated' attitude to employment will be encouraged in every type of school. Nor are these simply changes at the level of policy, ideas on paper. Goaded by government pressure, a new kind of teaching has emerged, that incorporates aspects of progressive education while abandoning its supposedly eccentric social commitments. This pedagogy is student-centred, activity-based, proud of its relevance. It contrasts itself with the academic and book-based character of traditional models, and adds evidence to the claim that a break with the past has at last been made.

In these ways, it is said, and with this attention to detail, the bias of a century is being corrected.

But what is new or distinctively Conservative about all this? 'Education for the world of work' was, after all, a favourite slogan of the last Labour government; it was James Callaghan who criticized schools for their emphasis on the 'social' rather than the 'economic'. Even now, these themes are a staple element in Labour's discourses on education. So aren't they signs of the times, and not the property of any one party?

If we ignored the special fervour with which the Conservatives promote the entrepreneurial ideal, and if we set aside the decisiveness with which they have brought about changes in institutions and systems of control, then the answer might be, yes. But even then, there would be a second tendency to take account of, another thread to the Tory project of demolition and reconstruction, which is entwined so closely with the stresses on the technological that it forms one strong and connecting skein.

The doctrine that underlay post-war reform held that economic progress depended upon a more general provision of a higher-quality education, and upon equalizing the opportunities available to students from different social classes. To this economic argument for equal opportunity was added another, that the interests of social justice compelled an increase in opportunity and an expansion of education. The arguments combined in a reforming advocacy that linked justice and efficiency, individual interest and economic need. Although we know now that the opportunities offered were for the most part seized by the less disadvantaged members of society, nevertheless this kind of understanding of reform had real effects. It suggested that the 'needs of the economy' could be met by an undifferentiated expansion of education – one which was not formally and deliberately targeted on particular manpower needs and particular social groups.

It is this position that the Conservatives are now dismantling. They reject the idea that a universal expansion of education is necessary to meet the needs they identify. They favour a much higher degree of targeting and selection: selection within schools, so as to maintain academic streams, and to develop technical ones; selection between schools, so as to build up centres of scholarly excellence or colleges of technology. In each case, it is implicit that there are groups who are not targeted for favourable treatment, for whom lower levels of education and different conceptions of relevance are proposed.

The second tendency, then, of Conservative policy is its

3

unashamed selectiveness. It has broken with those previous policies that claimed to be taking steps towards the universalizing of high-quality education. Selectiveness, together with the stress on 'technologizing' the school, forms a new development in English education: a project of modernisation that flies right-wing colours.

For sixty years, it was the reforming left that claimed for itself the role of modernizer. The 'secondary education for all' that was embodied in the 1944 Education Act had long been the slogan of the Labour Party. It was Labour which in the 1950s and 1960s voiced, all too imprecisely, the call for comprehensive reorganization, and fostered new kinds of curriculum development. Throughout these years, the policy of the Conservative Party, and of Conservative governments, was a reactive one: on occasions conceding change; on others defending private privilege or public selection, and warning of the threats that faced them. For so long was it the inert, the marginal, the stupid party in education that it is difficult now to appreciate its new role. Instead of change, some analysts look for continuity: there was selection in the past, and there is selection in their programme now; in Thatcherism Victorian values are reborn. This is to miss all that is different in the new programme. Selection in the past privileged relatively small groups: the system that the Black Papers advocated in the 1970s comprised only five to eight per cent of the state school population. Conservative policy now proposes several different types of selection, in a system that would involve the majority of the student population in schools for which their parents had opted, and which had, in turn, decided to select them. In this way, positive selection will not be limited to those near the apex of an educational pyramid, but will also involve a large middle sector.

Traditional isn't the right word for this system. It borrows, of course, justifications from the past. It incorporates elements of older selective systems: the grammar school will survive. But overall it is new, and in its newness corresponds to other developing features of the economy, and of class and political relations, in Mrs Thatcher's Britain. In this wider arena, too, groups once fairly homogeneous in their exclusion from wealth and their opposition to Conservatism begin to disintegrate and polarize, as the relative success of some draws them into the orbit of Conservatism, while a 'second nation' of the poor and marginal grows in number.

The second face of Janus

So far, the stress of the argument has rested on the modernizing aspects of the Conservative programme. But what of those aspects that might be thought archaic in their dislike of cultural change, and their hostility towards pluralism and tolerance, towards multi-ethnicity and sexual diversity – in short towards the whole business of securing, through a degree of integration, the acceptance by subordinate groups of the social order in which they are governed? Are they important structural elements of modern Conservatism – or is it that, like the facades of the new classicism in architecture, these aspects are only present as decorations that enable a populist appeal, without affecting the fundamentals of policy or the functioning of the system?

In fact, archaism is much more than a superficial part of the programme. It both facilitates the destruction of an earlier consensus, and builds its distinctive features into the structures of newly-emerging systems. In two important ways, the right – that agglomeration of tendencies which is to be analysed in the next chapter – has made its mark. First, there is its relentlessly polemical character, and its tireless searching after error and excess in the policies of opponents. Its target is the education system of the welfare state, and its intention to present it as a system that has escaped rational control. Manipulated for their own ends by those who work in it, education, especially under local Labour control, has become a nest of minority causes, which interfere with the rights and opportunities of the majority. In the 1960s, the right identified the first fruits of these minority enthusiasms in the decline of standards that allegedly arose from the abolition of the grammar school. Later, and with greater bitterness, it attacked the left's policies on race and gender: they led, it was claimed, to an undermining of family life and national identity. Their unnaturalness could only be sustained by programmes of indoctrination and petty repression.

These themes – of a breakdown in cultural transmission and

5

intellectual discipline – are potent ones. They have been exploited with verve and success. From its bases in pressure groups and think tanks, and its connections with government and the media, the right has been able to elaborate and diffuse its own ideas. It has combined intense exploitation of particular controversies, against a background of constant newspaper support, with swift action to fix in law the advantages that accrue from successful campaigns. In doing so it has brought a strong coercive streak to Conservative policy. Its pressure groups have organized to drive some topics, like 'peace studies', out of the curriculum; to prohibit, by law, teaching deemed to be partisan; to ban the use of certain books, such as the Institute of Race Relations' *How Racism came to Britain*; and to close down or deradicalize particular courses and projects, such as Brent's Development Programme for Race Equality (DPRE). By prompting media ridicule, the occasional outburst of parental rage and the use of government action, it has been able to block or render marginal the views and initiatives of opponents.

But there is more to this project than the quest for immediate political advantage. There is a second, profounder aspect of the right's success. It has been able to create a series of fixed reference points and interpretative devices, by means of which people caught up in disorientating processes of social change can establish new or strengthened kinds of allegiance or identity. In this context, the revival of family and nation takes on a new significance, as, outside its traditional heartland in the grassroots xenophobia of Conservative support, the right makes appeal to other major groupings. First, amid the dislocations of the inner cities, it has identified a newly disadvantaged sector – a white underclass, whose interests, it is claimed, the rainbow alliances of Labour's urban politics have systematically neglected. Secondly, it has targeted those sections of the skilled working-class, particularly in the boom areas of the English south-east, whose votes have sustained Conservative dominance. Already enjoying the fruits of economic growth, this group has also proved susceptible to the right's agitation on social issues: an opinion poll conducted for London Weekend Television in late 1987 found that more than forty per cent of white parents in the south-east favoured race-segregated schools.

6

Traditionalist cultural themes thus come into play as means of reinforcing tendencies towards 'segmentation' in the working class. The right did not create the processes which have led to deindustrialization of the cities, and to increased economic differentiation between different groups of workers. It has, however, made every effort to ensure that the increased fragmentation of working-class experience works to the advantage of Conservatism. It is in this light that ideological issues take on a new importance, as points around which can cohere senses of group identity that are also statements of difference from constituencies where Labour still gains habitual support. Archaic energies thus have their place in the making of a new social landscape.

The road to 1988: prelude

The scope, then, of Conservative educational politics is a wide one. Yet its creation – or in some aspects, re-creation – is a recent work. The Conservatives who took office in 1979 had no great heritage of right-wing government on which to draw. Their predecessors of 1970-4 were most remembered for the cuts which had gained Margaret Thatcher, as Education Secretary, the title 'milksnatcher'. In other areas, the government had little to add to, or take away from the consensus of the time. It had accepted the rapid growth of comprehensive schools, supported increases in nursery provision and brought out a White Paper, called *Education: A Framework for Expansion*, that was so conventional in relation to the received wisdom and so lacking in thought about changing social trends, as to have attracted the critical attention of the OECD.

Mrs Thatcher has since made no claim to this inheritance, and has seldom recalled her part in it. Her reference points were the interpretations of the Heath experience made by its right-wing critics, the most important of whom was Sir Keith Joseph. Joseph was the first of Heath's cabinet to convert to monetarism. He was also the first to identify the importance to the right of being able to politicize debate on social policy. So long as the party confined its attention to the economic field, it would not be able to compete with Labour. Only a wider focus could ensure political success. The effects of egalitarianism in education, the crisis in the welfare state, the threats that were being posed to choice and freedom – these were issues both important and politically exploitable. It was with this in mind that in 1974 Joseph set up the Centre for Policy Studies, a think tank intended to reshape the climate of opinion in Britain.

The founding of the CPS was a sign of an important shift in the general line of Conservative policy. But in the 1970s, at least, there was little need for the right to call upon the services of its new think tanks to develop ideas on education policy. In this area, Conservatives could draw on an already-existing body of work, which, under the new dispensation, could move centre-stage. In 1969, the first of the Black Papers on education had appeared. Over the next decade, they developed both a critique of educational reform and the outlines of an alternative system, as well as demonstrating the political usefulness of anti-egalitarian themes. It was in large part due to their campaigning that in the 1979 election, 'Educashun isn't working' became a credible Conservative slogan.

The work of the Black Paper activists is evaluated in some detail in the next chapter,a later chapter, but because it had such a potent influence on educational politics, and did so much to inspire the revival of the right, it is worth pausing at this point to outline the two key themes, of standards and of choice, that were elaborated in their publications. The first was vital in placing the supporters of the new comprehensive system on the defensive; the second in identifying the discontents of a particular social layer, and in channelling them towards an alternative.

Even though so much energy has flowed into the search for proof that, all things considered, the exam results of the selective schools were better than those of the new system, the debate on standards has never been merely a technical discussion about quantifiable levels of achievement. From the start, it has resounded with other themes. The alleged inability of comprehensive schools and progressive teachers to reproduce the standards of the previous system amounted to a breakdown in cultural transmission and to a betrayal of the past. Schools were no longer able authoritatively to pass on a body of knowledge and standards of behaviour. Those who administered the schools, or who laid down or implemented curriculum policy, were to blame for an accelerating loss of cultural cohesion. Through this argument, the issue of achievement in schools became linked with wider themes of order, change and renewal. At the same time, an alternative programme began to emerge, that saw 'parental choice' as a means of regulating the curricular and political excesses of state schooling. Each school should be made dependent for its survival on its ability to attract students, and the school system would be reorganized so as to remove all barriers to choice. From the last of the Black Papers, published in 1977, onwards, 'choice' became both the basis of a programme for the organization and resourcing of schools, and a means of shaping particular conceptions of the role of parents and of the family. They would be active and collaborative seekers-out of the best educational goods available. Reform would only interest them in so much as it increased the market value of their child's education. Thus, in pursuit of personal advantage, they would erase all signs of ruinous egalitarianism from the school system.

Ten years of intellectual work on themes like these meant that by 1979 the Conservatives had available to them a rich educational discourse that reached outwards from the school to connect with issues of family life and national culture. There had also developed a cadre of activist intellectuals of the right, who were by now experienced in a kind of agitational politics that relied for its effect, not on the findings of detailed research or academic study, but on the searching out of weakness in the positions of opponents, and in the sharp presentation of countervailing themes. 1974 belonged, it seemed, to a different epoch.

Taking over, settling accounts

On taking office, Mrs Thatcher's government found an education system that, in absorbing over fourteen per cent of GNP – three per cent more than defence spending – had made itself a prime target for monetarist attention, with a special focus on curbing local authority spending. But, as Keith Joseph had understood, the problems of education were more than financial. The culture of the system – its hegemonic ideas and organizing principles – needed changing. The drive towards modernization and international competitiveness that – at least

9

at the level of rhetoric – had been the grand design of post-war governments had more and more been thought to depend upon an increase in the opportunities available to working-class students, so that the human resources they embodied could be swept up in the expected new waves of economic growth. Comprehensive education was one outcome of this understanding of the needs of modernization; a second was the licensing of some measure of progressive reform in the curriculum. Progressivism, with its stress on the needs of the child and its commitment to teaching methods that overcame the cultural barriers between disadvantaged students and learning, seemed to be a necessary complement of organisational change.

It would be wrong, though, to think that the climate of those years was determined by minute and precise calculations of the relation between educational expansion and economic growth. Indeed, it could be argued that the calculations were never produced at all: that 'manpower' needs were never translated with any clarity into educational objectives. What helped to ensure that such cold figuring, with its implied assignment of students to particular occupational slots in an unequal division of labour, did not become central to educational planning was the active presence of other commitments and ideals. Among these was the combination of belief in equal treatment, objections to privilege, and protest at wasted potential that motivated the reform movement. This concern for social justice was rarely converted from a principle to a closely defined programme for reform – a failure which explains many of the subsequent problems of the comprehensive school. Yet it pervaded thought about education and provided a language in which to think its purposes. 'Disadvantage', 'the needs of all our children', a 'more equal society' were some of the mild but persistent themes of official, consensual policy statements. They represented the summation of a century-old concern of a section of the British intelligentsia that valued social unity and a liberal culture more than it appreciated economic growth. They also reflected, in distant and mostly unadmitted ways, the labour movement aspirations that underlay the settlement of 1944. Together, such influences hegemonized the official culture of British education; so that, to most professional opinion, some version of equal opportunity was second nature.

But this imposing edifice of policy was more fragile than would first appear. It was the product, less of a sweeping away of an ancien regime, than of a series of compromises with it. Church influence had been safeguarded by the 1944 Act. The Wilson government had cautiously approached the issue of ending private education, and then retreated from it. Large pockets of selective education remained within the state system, and even where the grammar school/secondary modern division had formally been abolished, it remained an active influence upon the curriculum. Higher education was still a system virtually closed to those from 'disadvantaged' backgrounds.

This persistent failure to challenge the most powerful aspects of the established system had important consequences for the future of reform. With so many inertial influences upon it, the curriculum remained in important respects unmodernized – science, for instance, was scarcely present in primary education. Moreover, there was no extensive rethinking of the curriculum to match the reorganization of secondary schooling along comprehensive lines: schools experienced no cultural revolution, and many teachers continued to work with deeply pessimistic assumptions about the possibilities of educating working-class students. The official culture of education may have been progressive, but in the classroom other tendencies persisted. As those writers realized, who, like David Hargreaves, later came to draw up a sympathetic balance sheet of reform, this failure ensured that for most students schooling remained an experience which made little connection with their lives, and from which they withheld their commitment. Equal opportunity was a slogan which stopped at the gates of the comprehensive school. For the most part, it did not extend to the curriculum, and it certainly did not inspire demands for mass access to higher education.

Nor was the post-1944 system more democratic than its predecessors. The control of schools still largely excluded parents: the proposals of an official committee that in the mid-1970s recommended increasing parental involvement in 'a new partnership for our schools' had not been put into practice. Most schools turned their faces away from the communities in which they were located. A DES report on *Educational Disadvantage*, which in 1972 made suggestions for change, found its views neglected. Discussion of curriculum matters was a professional preserve. 'The complex issues of curriculum development', said the National Union of Teachers (NUT) in 1978, should be left to teachers. In short, the system, though universally provided, offered few points at which parental or community interests could become involved in discussion either about general educational purpose, or about the day-to-day running of the school.

Finally, it was a system which, by the mid-1970s, was beginning to suffer internal stress. The difficulties of reform, in a period marked by the growing attentiveness of Labour governments to international financial pressures, were causing less a deeper radicalism than a loss of heart. Perhaps, mused James Callaghan in 1976, schools had over-emphasized their social role, at the expense of the economic. Perhaps progressive experiment – which was in reality scarcely commonplace – had gone too far. From now on the government should ensure that the demands of the 'world of work' were more securely established at the centre of education policy. With this analysis, the Labour government began to cut through the ideological nexus that had been at the centre of the case for reform, severing the links between progressive education and economic requirement that had underlain earlier policy, and beginning the break-up of the alliance between educational opinion and Labour politics that had secured and developed comprehensive reform.

This is not to say that the impetus for change had become completely exhausted. In some schools and local authorities the pace of progressive reform quickened in the late 1970s. Radical work on race and gender, for instance, actually increased after 1979. What it lacked, though, under Callaghan and under Mrs Thatcher, was a confirming echo in central policy, and authoritative political statements that attempted to explain and justify the work of schools to non-educational audiences. What took the place of firm defence and open self-criticism were defensive silences, or new policies that in crucial areas – standards, the world of work – conceded ground to the opposition, and made the work of further change in those areas that were still a target of equal opportunity policies harder to achieve. It was in these last years of Labour rule that for the first

time since 1944 the Conservatives were able to step outside the
ghetto of selective principles to claim the right to reshape the
whole system: it 'wasn't working'.

The historic programme of reform, then, had run into
difficulties on all fronts: it lacked popular appeal, but did not
satisfy the criticisms of industrialists and civil servants. It had
delivered neither a modern, nor a popular education. The
school was ripe for change, for other strategies of achieving
these long-sought goals. Yet Mrs Thatcher's first government
had no programme ready-made to deal with the range of issues
voiced by the system's critics, nor to convert agitation into
policies. For most of the previous ten years, the substance of
right-wing achievement on curriculum and school organization
had been polemical, nostalgic, headline-making, necessarily
lurid. As Ray Honeyford was later to note, it lacked any general
'theory' of comprehensive education and of alternatives to it. By
stages over the next decade such an understanding was
developed, and on its basis a programme and a strategy
constructed. By 1988 Conservative governments had accumulated a set of policies that were wide in their scope and
unmatched in their attention to detail. They covered issues of
curriculum content, of standards and assessment, of the control
of the teaching force, and the accountability and management of
schools; of the contribution of schools to the national culture,
and of their relationship to the world of work. Other
governments, of course, had approached these issues before.
What distinguished the Conservatism of the mid-1980's was its
increasingly comprehensive approach, its centralised attention
to the minute particulars of policy implementation, and its
insistence that education policy was an area of political
contestation, where the aims were to uproot established
interests and transform a whole system and culture of learning.

Although inspired in important ways by the thinking of the
right, this programme has not emerged from some central
planning unit, nor as the result of a grand political strategy, but
out of several interconnected pressures and tendencies. The
pace and the character of development owe as much to
opportunism and to the pressure of events as to prior
calculation. In some respects, policy has developed in partial
continuity with the past – the Callaghan-inspired initiatives of

the 1970s, for example, have been taken up and strengthened. In some areas, such as control of the teaching force, it has arisen as a means of achieving decisive resolution of a particular struggle. In others, policy has developed through the campaigning ability of the right to exploit particular controversies and to turn them to legislative advantage. The strength of a programme formulated in this way is its closeness, its 'organic' relationship to the course of events. Its potential weaknesses are its eclecticism and subjection to the conflicting pulls of its shaping forces. At several points in its development, the difficulties of a programme combined in haste from so many different sources have been revealed.

1979–81: beginnings

The manifesto of 1979 was, by later standards, a modest one, and where it promised most, it least delivered. Reflecting the middle-class parental campaigns of the previous decade, it offered repeal of legislation that would have abolished selection in the state system. It announced a few measures to increase parental choice. It proposed a new attention to basic skills and a national system of testing – a scheme that prefigured a much later future. It was virtually silent on issues of the world of work.

The proposals on testing would have led to an early confrontation with the entire educational establishment. Under the 'wet' Secretary of State, Mark Carlisle, there was little chance that they would be implemented. Instead, there was legislation on other issues that, with hindsight, seems like a tentative harbinger of future change. The areas that the Education Act of 1980 addressed were those that would also preoccupy later ministers, but their scope was narrower. The Assisted Places Scheme provided subsidies for students transferring from state schools to the private sector. In doing so, it inaugurated a search for new forms of selection that could develop alternatives to the comprehensive system, without facing it in open and uncertain battle for the restoration of the grammar school. The publication of schools' examination results increased the pressures on schools to conform to popular criteria of educational worth. So too, in principle, did the proposals to give parents the right of appeal against a council's choice of school for their children, and the power to send their children to school across Local Education Authority (LEA) boundaries. Here were the first signs of a consumer-driven system. But at the same time, the DES attempted to use its central influence to co-ordinate local curriculum development: LEAs were asked what they were doing to adapt to curricular aims that, by contrast with later guidelines, were fairly general in their formulation.

Apart from this, right-wing attention to the detail of education policy was still sketchy. In fact, the government at this stage allowed many of the characteristic themes of education reform to remain in place. The Warnock Committee of Enquiry into Special Educational Needs and the Swann Report on the achievement of ethnic minority students were allowed to complete their work, though many of their recommendations, were set aside. In this period, the government's attention, despite Joseph's message of the 1970s, was devoted primarily to financial questions, rather than direct issues of social policy. Monetarist thinking demanded deep cuts in public expenditure to lay the basis for long-term economic revival. Grants to local authorities were greatly reduced in the first two years of Conservative rule. Teacher numbers began to fall. A climate of austerity pervaded the schools, and produced the first signs of parental concern and of teacher militancy that were later to have significant effects.

Nevertheless, these early years established areas of concern that were to remain central to Conservative policy. The legislation and the administrative action of this period can now be seen as a first exploratory step to the fuller working out of a system in which central control was increased, and at the same time choice was given a greater role, both as a means of consumer control over education, and as a principle allowing greater selectiveness. Their reach, however, was more impressive than their grasp. It was one thing to identify parental choice as a principle central to the restructuring of education. It was quite another to find the practical mechanisms which could make it effective, or the political strategy that could make it a feasible option on a wide scale. The introduction of a 'right to appeal' against school allocation made little difference to the functioning of the system. In fact, the Conservatives had not yet imagined, in any practical sense, the full possibilities of an education that combined market principles with central control. It was true that Rhodes Boyson, in 1975, had argued that these should be the two pillars of a sound education system. But in the early 1980s, the working out of the details of such a vision still awaited its technicians. More importantly, political conditions made a project like Boyson's seem unrealistic. The years of Carlisle's Secretaryship were the low point of the government's fortunes. The recession was at its deepest. Austerity was unpopular. The cabinet was still packed with anti-monetarist sceptics – Carlisle himself among them until his dismissal in the autumn of 1981. Trade union militancy was still, in some sectors, high, and almost the entire educational world was hostile to the point of ridicule to the programme of the radical right. That this situation changed was the outcome of a number of different conflicts and strategies, few of which could have been foreseen at the time of Carlisle's first cautious steps. Foremost among them were the conflicts with local authorities and with the teaching unions that dominated the next few years. Almost as important, however, was the determination shown by Carlisle's successor, Keith Joseph, in creating a feasible set of national policies for the monitoring and control of teaching and learning.

Joseph's years: 1981–86

The Joseph years were those of a growing Conservative ascendancy. The economy was climbing out of recession. A free market approach to international trade and investment, major cuts in sectors of state spending, and an industrial policy that eliminated less profitable capital and assaulted union power all seemed to be delivering benefits. A series of adversaries – Argentinians, miners, local councils, the peace movement – was confronted and defeated. The distinctive features of Conservative economic restructuring – including privatization and enterprise zones like Docklands – began to fall into place. Opposition from the wet side of the Conservative Party died away, and the influence of new right ideas became more pronounced. There began a programme of reshaping social institutions, so as to fit them for their part in this new society. It is against this background that Joseph's long Secretaryship should be assessed.

His weaknesses were always obvious enough: a marked indecisiveness in moments of crisis; an inability to communicate in public; a tactical maladroitness that was sometimes an opponent's dream. All these qualities were shown in painful abundance during the teachers' pay disputes that punctuated his term in office. Yet at the same time it was Joseph who first presided over that detailed elaboration of policy that is the impressive feature of the later years of Conservative rule. From 1983 to 1985 two major speeches on the curriculum and the teaching force, and two White Papers on *Better Schools* and *Teaching Quality* outlined a systematic policy for the curriculum and its delivery. The DES took close control over the content of initial teacher training courses and, later, moved to exert a heavier influence over all in-service teacher training. In these, and other areas, detailed criteria and guidelines for syllabuses and statements of educational objectives began to appear. The national inspectorate, an autonomous body often unenthusiastic about DES policy initiatives, was jogged into producing policy documents in many curriculum areas. In the same period, Joseph permitted – and observed with increasing interest – the first direct vocational inroads to be made on the school system, through the Manpower Services Commission-funded (MSC) funded Technical and Vocational Education Initiative (TVEI). Later, he was to welcome it as a salutary shock to the established educational culture.

This assessment is one of the keys to understanding Joseph's sense of purpose. He saw Britain as a country let down by its intelligentsia, which had shunned the disciplines of productivity and competition to cultivate softer areas of interest. Education was implicated in this long process of betrayal. One of the tasks of Conservative policy was to liberate it from its intellectual captors: to saturate it with respect for enterprise; to shake teachers and administrators out of their old practices; to accept no longer the low standards which disabled the country in international competition.

His instrument of renewal, however, was not the uncertain discipline of the market, nor the unruly and hazardous enterprise of promoting a grassroots movement for educational

17

change. It was instead, unashamedly, the central apparatus of the state. Joseph the economic liberal introduced education to *dirigisme* with a vengeance. At times – as he made speeches on physics, on history and on geography, and contested in all these areas the dubious aspects of the received wisdom; as he scrutinized the syllabuses of every subject in the General Certificate of Secondary Education (GCSE), and sought amendment to those that displeased him; as he inquired of students in the schools he visited how effective was the work of their teachers – he resembled nothing so much as some modernizing and absolute monarch of the eighteenth century. In such a role he involved himself with every aspect of life under his rule, not trusting the forces at work in civil society to produce the necessary results. In this guise, too, he was no friend of the right. Although an instigator of the right's intellectual revival, he resisted implementing some of its favourite market-orientated proposals: despite the views of some of his advisers, he would not sanction schemes to replace state funding of LEAs by payment to every parent of an 'educational voucher' which could be used to pay towards the cost of whatever school, private or state, that the parent chose. And, though he monitored closely the content of the new GCSE examination to which he gave his approval in June 1985, he did not accede to the new right's criticisms that it reinforced all the worst tendencies of the teacher-dominated syllabuses of the past. Thus, demanding radical change, Joseph, the self-proclaimed believer in the 'blind, unplanned, unco-ordinated wisdom of the market', found himself relying on the existing educational apparatus to deliver it. *The Times*, disappointed with the consequences of this choice, concluded that he had 'too often been malleable at the hands of the vested intellectual interests which dominate educational thinking'. In reality, he had made a decision about the best means of modernizing the system – a decision which led him away from the panaceas of the right.

Yet, for all its prodigious scrutiny, there was something lacking or uncertain in Joseph's perspective. He opened up a road of major change, and moved some way along it, but there were a number of areas where his drive towards modernization was compromised by his sympathies with strains in educational culture that were not at all congruent with it. He drew back from measures that would have demolished finally the strong-points of the established system, and would have set up new and radically different relationships between government and curriculum, parents and schools, teachers and managers. He considered, and rejected, the idea of a national curriculum; he refrained from imposing new conditions of service upon teachers. Perhaps this diffidence sprang from a continuing philosophical conviction about the autonomy of social relationships from state power. Certainly, in other ways, Joseph retained some affinities with the right, and the more spectacular forms of its campaigning. He spoke several times of the Conservative mission to create a sense of the continuity and integrity of the national culture, and of what one newspaper summary of his views called 'the myths by which the British people live'. These concerns made him indulgent to some of the key themes of the cultural right. Thus his most sizeable contribution to issues of educational control was his stewardship of the 1986 Education Act. The Act – a carnival of reaction if ever there was one – began as a few simple and important measures to increase parental representation on governing bodies, but grew to encompass in slapdash and sometimes unimplementable ways most of the concerns of the right. It included the proscription of partisan teaching about political matters, the right of parents to withdraw their children from sex education, and the codification of police influence on schools – headteachers had to have regard to police representations about curriculum matters. In general the Act was the creation of the Tory backbenches rather than the leadership; its accent was upon restraining at local level the work of progressive schools, rather than establishing a national direction for the curriculum. Joseph, despite the drift of his own policy initiatives, let this legislation happen. Its localist emphasis was soon jettisoned by his successor.

The most important blind spot in Joseph's vision was on the issue of resources. While insisting on the need to raise standards, he was just as firm that this should be done without strain on existing levels of financing. This was not a tenable position. During his period in office, discontent with the funding of education grew in intensity, and the disparity between his high aims for the system, and his extreme reluctance to argue in favour of adequate resourcing for it became generally obvious. Annually, in the mid-1980s, the inspectorate produced reports that spoke of obsolescent buildings, shabby classrooms, inadequate resources and declining teacher morale. The long campaign over teachers' pay, which lasted – with a brief interlude – from 1984 to 1986, raised the issue of resources in the sharpest form, and to Joseph's lasting discredit. Throughout 1985, he was intransigent in his refusal, as paymaster of the local education authorities, to fund the concessions that would have brought about a settlement. At certain points, his interventions – suggesting for instance that teachers were 'mad' not to accept what was on offer – actually strengthened his opponents' resolve. Thus, though his attritional handling of the dispute eventually eroded teachers' resistance to a point that allowed his successor a speedy victory, it also brought public disquiet at the conduct of educational policy to a new height. By mid-1986, the teachers' action had brought the issue of resourcing to the front of the picture. Their campaign may not have won them direct support, but the crisis that it caused provoked parents' organizations to step up their criticism of government, and led to a widespread loss of confidence in its policy. His credibility weakened, Joseph resigned – the low point, apparently, of Conservative education policy. It seemed for a moment as if the old educational agenda – of funding to ensure equality of opportunity – had pushed out the new. Yet, shortly afterwards, the offensive against the old consensus resumed, with even greater force. This occurred under Joseph's apparently more liberal successor, Kenneth Baker.

Baker: a new high point

Baker had a reputation as a Conservative moderate. A former Parliamentary Private Secretary to Edward Heath, he had his roots in a less militant Conservative era. His first government post, as Minister for Information Technology, seemed to link him with tendencies of modernisation rather than political reaction, and his spare-time occupation as an anthologist of verse earned him further liberal credentials, since poetry and Thatcherism were not generally considered compatible.

These impressions were established, of course, largely at a symbolic level. Nevertheless, they had some basis in Kenneth Baker's history, and seemed at first to have some substance in relation to current events. In his first weeks in office, Baker sacked Stuart Sexton, one of the more market-orientated advisers at the DES, and told the House of Commons of his belief in 'a diffusion of power rather than a centralised system'. But those who took these actions to be signs of a general commitment to the historic and consensual principles of educational policy misled themselves. It was under Baker that the militancy of the official Conservative programme soon reached new levels. Under the 1987 Pay and Conditions Act, teachers had their conditions worsened and their negotiating rights taken away. At the same time, of course, this was also a removal of the responsibility that the co-ordinating bodies of local employers had for a long time taken, of negotiating pay and conditions with teachers at a national level. Yet, the centralization embodied in this Act was a mere foretaste of the powers assumed by Baker in the Education Reform Act of 1988.

The ERA intensified central intervention in the curriculum to a point which Joseph had neither wished nor dared to reach. It introduced plans for a national curriculum, that covered virtually everything that was taught to students during the compulsory period of schooling. It complemented the programmes of study which were to be stipulated by such a curriculum with plans for the establishment of detailed 'levels of attainment' that students should reach, and with universal systems of testing, for students aged 7, 11 and 14, to ensure the performance of the whole system. As the national curriculum was implemented during the early 1990s, it would ensure the conformity of teaching objectives to centrally-established criteria; it would to a very large extent limit local curricular autonomy, and would inevitably affect both the content and the method of education. As such, it was the single most powerful measure of centralization in half a century. But it was by no means the whole of the ERA.

Baker had spoken of a 'diffusion of power'. In a certain sense, the Act delivered that diffusion. It used the central power of legislation to undermine the system of local authority-controlled education, and to create in its place a framework that – by the time of its full introduction in the mid-1990s – would give greater autonomy to individual schools, and that in so doing would strengthen the selective principle. Admission levels for schools were reset, so that the more popular institutions could expand. This also entailed, of course, the threat that schools which failed to become popular would face closure. Inexorably, a system of parental choice would widen differences in reputation, intake and resources between schools, and create a system, based on a degree of competition for entry into the popular schools, which was in fact, if not in name, selective. It would not be a simple re-creation of the grammar school/secondary modern divide which proved so unpopular with parents, but rather a more complex, multi-levelled hierarchy, that involved a greater diffusion of privilege, while retaining and strengthening the academic pinnacles of the system. Public schools and grammar schools would remain. Schools where parents voted to leave the locally-controlled system could do so. They would be funded by the central state, controlled by their governors, and left free to seek further financing from local business, and to attract the students they thought suitable. In opting out, they would join outside the local system a further tier of education: the 'City Technology Colleges', selective schools in city areas, part-funded by business.

At the same time, the Act introduced a new method of allocating and controlling school finances. Local authorities would no longer have the discretion to fund smaller schools at a more generous level than others. A school's revenue would depend very largely on the number of students it could attract: 'think of each pupil as a bag of cash' a DES official told educationists who had come to hear more about the early stages of the scheme. The new system, 'Local Management of Schools' thus placed a quasi-market pressure on the school to attract the maximum number of students. Once funds were allocated to the school, it would be for the governors to decide how to spend them. Their priorities, in a market situation, would be very different from those of an LEA. They would exert a further downward pressure on the conditions of those who worked in schools, and encourage a close attention to public relations, marketing and financing.

Baker had thus both increased central influence in curriculum matters, and opened up the administration of schools to a version of market forces. He had developed and in most respects surpassed Joseph's attentiveness to the detailed functioning of the school system, and set out a policy that reached into its every corner. A long distance had been travelled since the first tinkerings of 1979. To explain why the final, swiftest and longest stage should be travelled by the 'moderate' Baker, rather than by his apparently more committed predecessor is to grasp much that is revealing about contemporary Conservatism.

One answer lies in the rapidity and creativeness of new right thinking between the elections of 1983 and 1987. It succeeded in outlining credible alternatives to a system which was not responding enthusiastically to the demands of a new era. In 1984, the *Omega File* of the Adam Smith Institute had presented a blueprint for a reorganization based on market principles, with a supporting role for a national regulation of minimum standards. A similar approach was outlined in the proposals of the No Turning Back group of Conservative MPs in 1985, and in 1986 by the Hillgate Group of Roger Scruton and his co-thinkers. These different contributions, though varying in the stresses they placed on free market economics as against cultural continuity, formed a consensus on the right that was in agreement around the broad outlines of a radical policy. Yet, important though it was, this focused unity cannot alone explain why selectiveness, and the market principles on which it is based, came to dominate the Conservative educational programme.

The most important factor in the radicalizing of education policy was the overall development of Conservative strategy. The pattern of economic recovery, out of the depths of recession, had revealed to Conservatives social tendencies that were swiftly converted into political gains. Growth was, more than ever, a selective phenomenon. The older industrial sectors, propelled by government policy, went into sharp, perhaps irreversible decline: coal, steel and shipbuilding shed jobs by the hundred thousand. Growth was concentrated in particular sectors: services, banking and finance, self-employment and the 'microchip industries'. It was these sectors, where workers were relatively secure in their prospects, and were experiencing real gains in their standard of living, that provided an extended base for the Conservative Party – so much so that in the south of England a high density of industry now correlates with electoral support for the Tories. Conservative policies have been assiduous in nurturing this base. It has been showered in gold from tax-cuts, from share purchases in privatized utilities, and capital gains in a buoyant and heavily subsidized housing market. The price of this nurturing has been paid by what remains of public sector industry, the underfunded welfare state, and by the poor, who have lost billions in benefit.

On the basis of these two profoundly divergent and polarizing tendencies, the Conservatives have constructed a 'two nations' political economy. Employment and housing increasingly reveal a pattern in which a large core of skilled, full-time, home-owning workers is surrounded by a periphery of low-paid or semi-employed millions. This is something more than the old distinction between private affluence and public squalor: it creates, not so much a distinction between a rich elite and the excluded masses, as a sharpened differentiation within the working population. Its political effects, Conservatives hope, will be to create a constituency so thoroughly implicated in the benefits and market procedures of Thatcherism that it will forever associate its security and welfare with the pursuit of private advantage, and will accordingly forsake its interest in the fate of collective provision.

It is this approach which has now been set to work in education. Home and share ownership, Mrs Thatcher argues, were among the strongest political bases for Conservative success in the 1987 election. By 1991, she states, education will have been added to the list. In keeping with the larger model, choice, selection, differentiation and inequality will form its basic pattern, but its mechanisms for the creation of advantage will be more flexible than in the past, and the target groups which it privileges will be larger.

So, in the most important sense, there was no mystery in Baker's sponsorship of the ERA. He was both riding a wave of educational opinion within the Conservative Party, and furthering the general line of the Conservative programme as a whole. His legislation dramatized a general evolution of the

24

contemporary right, in which Baker, as much as any other Cabinet minister with a career to think of, was caught up. In this process, the gifts of emollience and public reasonableness that were once applied to negotiate compromise could be employed to present consensus-breaking and authoritarian policies in reassuring guise. He was no exception to the general government attitude to issues of democracy. He shared its harsh way with trade union opposition and the narrowness of its conception of legitimate dissent. The policies which embody these attitudes, however, were ones that he presented with a flair for public relations, a sense for the weaknesses of opponents, and an ability to dominate the middle ground. Both the authoritarian substance of his policy and the political skills of its presentation could be seen in his handling of the teachers' dispute.

Baker came to office in May 1986, just as the teachers' campaign – with its periodic strikes, refusal to cover for absent teachers, and refusal to attend meetings after school or write reports – had begun to wear itself out. Although it was strong enough to disrupt the functioning of schools and wring some minor gains from government and employers, the very length and obduracy of the campaign had seen a certain draining away of public support. Earlier in the year, the main parents' organization had called for the action to stop. A traditional, tacit closeness between the NUT and the Labour Party had almost broken down, as Labour councils moved to discipline teachers and in negotiations demanded drastic changes in their working practices. Generally, the action, which had rendered much of the normal work of the school difficult to carry out, had added to a pervasive sense among one-time supporters of reform that the possibilities of a whole period had now been exhausted. Professional autonomy, far from speeding the pace of relevant and exciting change, had led only to an educational graveyard of strikebound inactivity. Now, on top of these serious general problems, the various unions were split on matters of tactics and of principle. The second-biggest union, the National Associa-tion of Schoolmasters/Union of Women Teachers (NAS/UWT), had in March agreed to call off action in return for an interim pay award, and the commencement of talks that would trade off extra pay for worse conditions. In April, the

25

NUT, isolated, had just agreed to join the other unions in these negotiations, that were soon to lead to concessions that disheartened many of its most committed members.

This was a situation tailor-made for Baker's decisive intervention. Counter-attacking, he was able to codify and to an extent popularize the lessons of the action: teachers, professional people allegedly, had walked out on their responsibilities and disrupted the education of millions. It was another sign of a rot within the system, another argument for change. But the opportunity could be turned to more than a rhetorical advantage. Eventually, in the autumn of 1986, the teachers, led by the NUT, reached an agreement with their employers, that conceded management control of conditions in return for quite substantial increases in pay. At this point, Baker had a choice. He could either accept the deal, as embodying the teachers' acceptance of their weakened position, or he could use their disarray as the occasion for a crushing advance. The first option left open the possibility that teachers could claw their way back to a position of influence. The second meant total victory, but at the expense of alienating a great number of teachers, and of making less likely their co-operation with whatever projects of educational change he might decide to introduce.

A few months earlier, Joseph had made known his unhappiness with 'the idea of compulsion in relation to teachers' duties'. But by now the conflict had gone on too long, and the blueprint for education on which Baker's civil servants were now working did not in any case envisage a strong creative or participatory role for teachers. Baker thus overturned the agreement that the teachers and their employers had reached, and imposed his own variant: worsened conditions, smaller pay increases and the abolition of negotiations. Till further notice, pay and conditions would be determined by an advisory body, appointed by himself. Teachers' unions could make representations to this body, but not negotiate with it. Local authorities would be cut out of the picture. Thus, out of confrontation had emerged, through opportunism and design, a set of measures appropriate to the overall drive of Conservative policy.

As with the unions, so with the curriculum. Basic to the government's approach was an hostility towards customs of local autonomy or professional influence that placed a check on its reforming zeal. To this extent, intolerance was part of its programme. But it was further fuelled by a series of sharp conflicts between the government and local councils, that began over issues of financing, and spread to cover the efforts of some Labour councils to make the Town Hall a base for developing alternative economic and social policies. The problems that faced these councils were many. Government cuts were severe, and the councils' efforts to cope with them gave rise to many strains. Ratepayers protested as councils sought to raise local revenue to compensate for government underfunding. Trade unions took action against cuts in services that the councils passed on. From the early 1980s onwards, local government was in crisis.

This was the unfavourable context in which were put forward new projects for race and gender equality that in some cases challenged the educational practices of many years, and the beliefs of centuries. The content and difficulties of these projects are material for another chapter. It is enough to note here the way that they were exploited by the right and by the government. Centralism found a new justification. Labour could be presented as the mere defender of minority causes, which had no purchase on the major issues of the educational agenda. Where these causes were not irrelevant, they were positively malign in their effects on family life and cultural cohesion. In this attack on 'loony leftism', ministers increasingly drew their weapons from the armoury of right-wing thought: the ideas of culture and nation developed on the right became central to the offensive against Labour in local government. Race and sexuality became front-line political issues.

Keith Joseph had certainly been attuned to issues of culture and nation. Baker equalled him, though, in the depth of his nationalism and surpassed him in converting belief into political tactics. 'Fundamentally a blood and soil nationalist', wrote Tom Paulin, reviewing his anthology of English history in verse – an overstated judgement, but one which picked out, nevertheless, a particular thread of Baker's interest in language and history. It is an interest which he has not hesitated to make known to the educational world and to urge on curriculum planners. More immediately important, though, was his collusion with the media's use of the cultural themes of the right against local

27

authority policies, in order to make a general case against anti-racism in education. What established its credibility was a succession of incidents in the London Borough of Brent in the autumn of 1986. First was the suspension of a primary headteacher, Maureen McGoldrick, against whom, the council said, there was prima facie evidence of racially discriminatory remarks. By first referring the case to her school governors and then, when they had cleared her, by taking the matter to another disciplinary body, the council managed to obscure issues of anti-racist policy in furious arguments about the irregularity of its procedures. In defence of their member, the NUT organized local strikes and took action in the courts. The ruinous tensions between a local council with progressive policies and the main teachers' union were exposed for all to see. To council supporters, the union was racist. To the union the council's attitude was 'McCarthyite'. Amid this conflict, Baker, in eventually intervening to reinstate Ms McGoldrick, was able to present himself as a moderating influence, whose concern was to protect the rights of the individual against a new oppressive zealotry.

The impression thus gained was swiftly exploited. Local authorities with large numbers of ethnic minority students are eligible for a grant from the Home Office to provide an education suitable to their needs. Originally, these needs had been defined as centring on the learning of English, but Brent had used the money to set up its 'Development Programme for Race Equality', that planned to employ nearly 200 teachers to reshape the work of its schools. In this way the curriculum could be stripped of what the programme called its 'Eurocentric' assumptions, and the levels of achievement of ethnic minority students, who formed a neglected majority of the school population, could be raised. In October 1986, buoyant in the wake of the McGoldrick affair, the *Mail on Sunday* launched an attack on the programme. Its staff were 'race spies in the classroom', 'thought police'. The whole project was 'Orwellian' in its efforts to monitor and influence the work done in Brent schools. The following spring, a BBC *Panorama* documentary on Brent, shot like a film noir, with supporters of Brent's policies filmed in the shadows, through bars or wire mesh, further developed the themes of extremism and oppression. By

28

mid-1987, election-time, Baker could confidently refer to Brent as an area where parents would leap at the chance to opt out of the local authority system, and much of the case for the national curriculum could be made to rest on the alleged extremism of Labour councils.

Brent, then, indicated in the clearest terms a government attitude to curriculum reform in 'controversial' areas, as well as demonstrating that it was willing to use curriculum issues as counters in a wider political game. During and after the Brent affair, Baker showed himself adept at utilizing opportunities provided by right-wing and media campaigns to increase the pressure on local authorities and to maintain an ideological offensive. Thus, after protests organized in 1987 by the right-wing 'Committee for a Free Britain' against positive images of lesbians and of gay men in the curriculum of the London Borough of Haringey's schools, he asked his inspectors to investigate; while his government introduced, in Section 28 of the Local Government Act of 1988, a ban on the local authority 'promotion' of homosexuality. Likewise, later that year, when the *Sun* revealed that teachers at a London primary school had organized an assembly on the occasion of Nelson Mandela's birthday, the national inspectorate were quick to arrive in its classrooms.

In these ways, Baker helped instil if not a great fear, then at least a great caution, among educators. Schools had to beware of questioning received ideas. Councils had to think twice before turning their attention to newly-recognized areas of discrimination. Around the new network of 'positive' state powers developed a negative climate of banning and deterrence.

Tensions

If Baker, then, was a moderate, his moderation was strictly relative to the rightward-moving consensus within Conservatism. With the passing of the ERA, he increased both the central authority of the state, and empowered groups of parents to take advantage of opportunities for local autonomy. By mid-1988, he commanded more statutory power than any Education Secretary before him. He had accomplished a drastic reduction in trade union rights and influence. He had overseen and encouraged a narrowing of ideas of the educationally permissible. And he had combined the centralizing tendencies of Joseph with a reshaping of school organization and financing that gave a greater weight to market forces.

Yet for all this, there remain important tensions at the heart of Conservative policy which explain why Baker, the minister who had made a reality of so much of the right's programme, was still so widely distrusted by it. In the vision of radical Conservatives, the school system would be almost entirely shaped by the play of parental choice. The pressures of the market place would hold in check the excesses of reform, while necessitating a continual benign product innovation in the curriculum. To this extent, the educational market would regulate itself. For Baker, this programme was insufficient. It threatened to produce the kind of unregulated system that, with its substantial pockets of blatant underachievement, would bring the whole programme of change into disrepute. Just as importantly, the imperatives of international economic competition demanded that a strong central hand should take hold of education and shake it into sensing new priorities and the need for higher standards. For this task, the market was too weak an instrument, and the curriculum ideas of the new right were too antiquated to be of use. Instead, Baker, like Joseph before him looked to a different source of support. He returned to a section of the educational establishment, and sought their help in devising the programmes of study and the targets of assessment that were essential to the national curriculum. Nowhere else could he have found a detailed concern with what a 'modernized' education system entails. The right regarded this as a betrayal. The very experts whose influence they had set out to curtail were now being invited through the front door of the DES to devise a curriculum for all state students! The simple proposals of the right were being magicked into a system of learning and assessment that repeated the detested catch-phrases of the 1960s about an 'activity-based, student-centred' curriculum. It was not surprising that a spate of pamphlets from the Centre for Policy Studies warned that the sharp edge of change was being blunted by Baker's reliance on the functionaries of the ancien regime.

Underlying these arguments were important differences about the nature and direction of Conservative education policy. It is to the roots of these differences that the next two chapters turn.

2

Tradition and the market

This chapter examines two tendencies in the thought and politics of the right. The first could be termed 'cultural rightism'. It could trace its philosophy back to Hobbes and its political ideology to Burke. It emphasizes the importance of a strong state to control the evils that an unregulated society is prey to. It regards custom and tradition as vital properties of an established order. Without them, the state is weakened, and subversion can grow in strength. Thus it regards cultural cohesion as an essential prop of state authority.

The second tendency is a continuation of classical liberal thought. Whatever is good in society comes about through the interaction of free individuals. If the state intervenes to regulate their relationship, it will produce a range of evils, that stretches from bureaucracy and economic inefficiency to totalitarian oppression. This principle applies as much to social questions as to the economic transactions of the free market which provide the inspiration for this kind of liberalism. The most efficient system, and the one which provides the greatest opportunities to the greatest number, is one which does not seek to control individual initiative.

In the abstract, these two currents of thought would seem to be deeply antagonistic: one is plainly authoritarian; the other celebrates unconfined individualism. Their present interconnectedness is a consequence of the historical problem which they both seek to resolve. Their common features begin with an attempt to understand, and to turn to political advantage what Andrew Gamble has called the 'breakdown of authority and stability in the world system and in national politics'. In the decade after 1968, the international system that had been for twenty-five years guaranteed by the strength of the United States was placed under immense strain. One aspect of this strain was military: the rise of the Soviet Union to a position of

32

near-comparability with the West and the defeats suffered by Western states and their proxies in South-East Asia, Africa and Central America. Another was economic: the oil price rise, the collapse of currency stability and the recession of the mid-1970s made clear the precariousness of Western prosperity. Politically, the period saw increasing conflict within Western societies, as large groups of workers, and students, challenged in spectacular ways both the austerities that accompanied the long boom's ending, and, to an extent, the hegemonic ideologies of the post-war era.

Left and right

These crises met with responses from the left as well as the right. If it was the former which first held the attention, it was the latter which proved in the longer term more capable of changing the situation whose problems they analysed. Since the right has both learned from and tried to bury the work of the left, and since a recurring sub-theme of this book is an attempt to explain and to alter the left's record of increasing ineffectiveness, it is worth taking time here to set out some of the ways in which the post-1968 left understood the situation before it, and the kind of programme it formulated in response.

For the left, 1968 and after were years of hope. Capitalist society seemed to have become fragile from the blows which were shaking it. Expectations were high that social democracy's role in defending a system which was so stultifying of creativity, and so plainly unable to deliver the economic rewards which it once had promised, would lead to a mass, leftward-moving rejection of its policies and leaderships.

Much of the left's critique centred on the work-processes of mass production society – of what one Parisian poster called 'les cadences infernales' of the assembly line. These were the basis of a society that stunted individual potential and created profound inequalities. It was a society whose governing institutions offered to the mass of people only the shadow of democracy – a vote every five years. Real social change would entail reorganising the work processes, reshaping relations between the sexes, and establishing institutions that guaranteed authentic popular control over the processes that affected the lives of most people. From these starting points arose a very rich and varied critique of the mid twentieth-century world – its ideologies, economic arrangements and political systems. The programme and practice of social democratic parties came in for particular criticism, and there were many who wished either to break their monopoly hold over working-class political representation, or to transform them into radical, socialist parties.

These ideas and aspirations did not, however, become politically hegemonic. The main reason for their eclipse was the power of political forces and traditions which they did not have the social weight to influence. The newly-born left could criticize a Wilson, a Mitterrand, or a Schmidt, but simply had not accumulated the levels of support necessary either to pressure, or to replace them. Nor did the difficulties of social democracy in office provide the hoped-for opportunities. Relatively weak as it was, the left had no choice but to suffer, along with the very parties which it criticized, the effects of general disillusionment with the performance of social democracy in government.

There were other reasons, too, for its ineffectiveness – reasons, that, paradoxically, are bound up with its very successes. The left, or, more precisely, the 'social movements' of the seventies, made their major advances when they forced previously 'marginal' issues – such as those associated with race and sexuality – onto the agenda of the labour movement, and to more general social attention. The problem was that these achievements were not accompanied by the presentation of an 'all-round' political programme, that addressed general issues of democracy or economic strategy. This weakness was a result of social implantation and political orientation – the left had little practical experience of the economic issues that naturally occupied the labour movement, and was generally more attuned to an international revolutionary tradition than to the specifics of national development. Its outcome was that the parts of the left's programme – its necessary stresses on gender and race and internationalism , for instance – came to stand for the whole. It seemed not to possess a set of policies – only a general ideological position, and a collection of views on particular individual issues.

This is not to say that the left did not have a wider social influence. Some of its attitudes, connected with the critique of mass-production society, passed into general circulation. The counterposition of imagination and creativity to the deadening routines imposed by the factory, and the setting of small-scale, co-operative activity against the soulless corporation became familiar cultural motifs. But, as will become clear, it was precisely these more diffused effects of '1968' which were most vulnerable to being absorbed by other, opposing ideologies..

The political record of the right – in Britain, at least – is stronger. In part, this is because it has been carried on the back of stronger forces: economic restructuring, for instance, has prevailed over trade union resistance. It is also the case that the right is guaranteed the support of most of the press. Even so, it can in important respects outmatch its opponents. It is much more successful in addressing what Gramsci called the 'decisive economic nucleus' of hegemony: the programme it has helped inspire offers clear definitions of the British crisis, and solutions to it that have brought measurable benefits to a substantial part of the working population. On other issues – more 'social' than 'economic' – the right's campaigning, with media assistance, has been much bolder and clearer than that of its opponents. It has spoken with assurance in defining the 'national culture', and in appealing to national tradition, confident that challenges to its interpretations are socially marginal. On this basis, it has identified targets for attack and elaborated ideological themes with a clear sense of the ideas that will relate to particular, well-rooted national attitudes: the exploitation of racist themes is a case in point. By contrast, the left and social democracy lack a well-developed economic programme, a clear sense of what has to change in British society, and an image of the kind of society they each want to create.

In the early 1970s, many on the right shared the left's expectations of turmoil to come. The apocalyptic tone of *The Times*'s editorials in 1974, after the miners' second strike, and the election of a Labour government, is among the most vivid reminders of that great fear. But fear did not lead to paralysis. Whereas the industrial militancy of these years failed to convert itself into a radical political challenge, the right was able to utilize its worries to generate the kind of nervous energy that could inspire new programmes and activities, and turn the crisis in the post-war settlement to its own advantage. It became plain after the slump of 1974 that the possibilities of the post-war system were becoming exhausted. As Gamble puts it, the check to demand and confidence integral to the recession 'dramatically exposed the obsolescence of many established industries. Investment opportunities in many fields had become saturated. In many industries it was difficult to make any further gains in productivity with the existing technology.' What was required was a major restructuring of the world economy, with the 'disappearance of a large part of existing employment and the introduction of new technological systems'. Attendant on these policies would be a drastic remoulding of state expenditure, so as to transfer benefits away from lower-income groups towards private capital and the better-off. This perception – which was not of course the outcome of some conspiratorial meeting, but of a general economic logic and its reflection in the programmes of business leaders and political parties – led to a radical change of attitude to social democracy. From being a pillar of stability, essential to the system, it became seen as a major contributor to political and economic crisis. In adopting measures to lessen disadvantage, to expand the public sector, and constrain the influence of market forces, social democracy, whatever its mildness, had erected institutional barriers to economic restructuring and encouraged popular attitudes which were unconducive to it. Like the post-1968 left then – though for entirely different reasons – the right developed an offensive against social democracy. In this context, both 'free market' and 'cultural' thought found a place. The former tendency was relentless in its criticism of public sector inefficiency, of government regulation, and of the economic costs of trade unionism. It was also fertile in its proposals for economic restructuring. Schemes for privatizing the public monopolies and local council services flooded from free market think tanks. Their ideas gave a new impetus to anti-union laws, and to the removal of safety and minimum wage protection for sections of the workforce. But they also contributed to a more pervasive social effect. Bureaucracy and economic stagnation, they argued, shackled the individual's potential for development. There were millions who could benefit, personally and financially, from the opportunities that would arise in an enterprise economy, liberated from what one free market pamphlet, impudently recycling the imagery of 1968, called 'the ideology of the production line economy, with standardised institutions turning out standardised services for standardised people'. The future belonged to those who recognized that the day of the production line economy was over. 'Now, there are new models, with smaller units of organisation, and more temporary relations and associations to bind them'. These new models of economic organization offered an escape from the old world. It was necessary to apply them not merely to private industry, but to the public sector and the welfare state as well. Notions of universal provision and of control by the bureaucracies which provided it should be discarded, so as to allow private initiative to find new ways of meeting consumer demand.

In this kind of rhetoric, the free market right was responding to the tensions identified in the post-68 critique. It joined in the attacks on the production line, celebrated the potential of the individual, and suggested new futures for the world of work. In doing so, one of its aims was to recuperate and thus to nullify some – if not all – of the aspirations to which 1968 did make appeal. The challenge of that year was taken up, but in a way which entirely dismissed demands of a democratic kind, and which revelled in new inequalities of provision.

However, the problems of those parties and interests wishing to overturn the post-war settlement were not confined to the areas addressed by free market thought.

Many tendencies of post-war economic growth – mass immigration from the third world, for instance, or women's entry into the paid workforce, or the abolition of the grammar school – had worked to weaken some of the values and habits which had been useful to the reproduction of the established order. The free market celebration of change and movement did little to quell these dangers. Nor did it do enough to address the themes of social authority which would be necessary to legitimize tough treatment of resistance to rightward change. For these reasons, the picture of dynamic escape from the old mass-production world was supplemented in the overall programme of the right by an authoritarian social philosophy: an appeal to tradition and continuity; a restatement of older, hierarchical values against the cultural disintegration and malevolent modernity which in the last years of the post-war boom were allowed to thrive. If one aspect of the right's thought, then, sought to *absorb* some of the impulses of 1968, this second aspect aimed to stifle them.

In formal terms, these two tendencies are contradictory, and at points their contradictions have recognisable effects at the level of policy and action. In reality, however, they generally complement each other, even to the extent of inhabiting the mind of the same individual. In education, figures for the most part associated with the cultural right, such as Baroness Cox, and the ex-headteacher Laurie Norcross, can appear as authors of free market publications, and the models of school organization worked out by libertarian think-tanks can swiftly be adopted by 'cultural' thinkers like Roger Scruton. Jointly, they have popularized the most powerful theme of right-wing educational discourse: that the decades-long quest for equality has resulted only in a lowering of standards. Cultural analysis of what Scruton calls the 'impractical utopian values that will destroy all that is most valuable in our culture', and free market assertion about the evils of state monopoly combine to add solidity to a central case: equality is the enemy of quality and of democracy. It has reduced standards, damaged the interests of the able student, licensed all sorts of eccentric reform and diminished the possibilities of parental choice. In short, the combined attacks on the alleged effects of equal opportunity have been invaluable to a programme that seeks to transfer resources and opportunities away from disadvantaged groups. When Kenneth Baker, introducing the Education Reform Bill to the House of Commons, asserted that standards, choice and freedom were indivisible, it was the varied and persistent efforts of the right that gave authority to his claim.

Developing the Right: the Black Papers

The new right in education was not born from Keith Joseph's conversion to market principles, nor even with the revival of 'cultural' and nationalist rightism that has been so important to the Conservative Party since the later 1970s. Its origins lie further back, beyond the post-1974 seachanges, in a miscellany of discontent, not all of it Conservative in origin – with the educational reforms of the 1960s.

In 1969 was published the first of a series of essays on the perils of educational reform. It achieved instant notoriety and a wide readership. *Fight for Education: A Black Paper*, edited by two university teachers of English, identified in the changes of the 1960s a threat to educational standards and discipline. Progressive educational methods, officially sponsored by government reports, were lowering standards of achievement in basic skills and weakening the authority of teachers. The rapid expansion of comprehensive schools, together with a growth in unstreamed teaching, was eroding the values of discipline, self-improvement and hard work that had been developed in the grammar school. In addition, while schools were being thrown into turmoil by hasty and unjustified reform, higher education was facing an even greater threat, in the form of a barbarous and anti-educational student militancy.

These assertions articulated the attitudes of many Conservatives to educational change, and represented the surfacing of a subterranean discontent with the consensus of party leaderships around reform. Yet none of the first three Black Papers, from 1969 to 1971, expressed an explicit orientation towards the reshaping of Conservative policy. Their editorials made calls on Labour Party moderates to restrain an extremist leadership, bent upon total comprehensivization. Their readership, it was claimed, belonged to no particular political constituency but were 'mainly teachers', who 'greeted with enthusiasm' the first Black Paper. Most teachers, it was argued, 'feel streaming is essential'. They realised that the Education Secretary, 'Mr Short, has gone too far'. There were, of course, progressive teachers, just as there were doctrinaire educationists and extremists in the Labour Party, but on the whole, in the opinion of the Black Papers, the mainstream of educational opinion was of sound mind and sceptical disposition.

In keeping with this analysis, the programme of these early papers was a limited one. It was a matter of defending 'excellence' by maintaining the public schools, alongside a strong but relatively small grammar school sector. The pace of reform would be slowed and progressive teaching methods introduced in a more cautious and experimental way.

It would be a mistake, though, to read the early Black Papers as a set of policy proposals. At least as important as their political programme was their ideological impact. In their attention to some of the real difficulties of reform, and to commonplace fears about what was happening in an education system suddenly become strange, they brought into question some of the prevailing assumptions about the benefits of change, and replaced them with a sense of crisis. The ending of selection and the decline in standards put at risk society's ability to pass on the cultural values of the past. Far from uniting society at a higher level of achievement, reform, by weakening authority and eroding the common stock of cultural meanings, was creating a crisis of order – one of whose first symptoms was the student militancy which followed university expansion.

The experience out of which the Black Papers grew was undoubtedly the partial abolition of the grammar school and the middle-class anxieties to which it gave rise, but always, within the argument, there was room for a special stress on the frustration of the abilities of working-class students, for whom the grammar school had offered far more of an opportunity for individual advancement than the comprehensive ever would. It was this claim that gave the first Black Papers a special power. Though throughout the educational world their views were treated with a foolish superciliousness, as irrelevant to the experience of reform, in fact they had identified frustrations and disappointments that were endemic in the new system. The comprehensive dawn had not brought in a widespread rethinking of the education needed in a common school. The secondary system was a *mélange* of the occasional bold experiment, some piecemeal reform, and a simple retention of older methods, derived from selective schools. Moreover, it had developed procedures and habits which made plausible the Black Papers' charge that it seemed to glory in its non-accountability. Education, they could allege, had become a vast 'interest' in which the concerns of educationists, administrators and politicians had developed their own dynamic, which steamrollered on, over the experiences and views of students, teachers and parents. It was this curricular incoherence and apparent lack of accountability, which gave relevance to the older certainties of the Black Papers. For the first time in decades, it became possible for the right to speak of state education with authority and verve, to link concern for state schooling with a critique of the direction and consequence of reform. In doing so, it achieved considerable resonance: the first two Black Papers sold 80,000 copies, becoming the first popular and effective critique of the post-war welfare state.

The success of the Black Papers was not simply a matter of the cogency of an argument – still less of its precision. Many of their specific claims about a decline In standards were refuted, in books like Nigel Wright's *Progress in Education*. But these claims were never essential to the Black Papers' popular impact: their success was a matter of finding a language in which change could be evaluated, and fragmentary dissatisfactions brought together. They enlisted the disillusioned voice of experience, that dramatized and personalized a social process, and helped establish the credibility of the claim that something had gone badly wrong with the whole project of reform. Cox and Dyson, editors of the early Black Papers, had themselves both voted Labour in 1966. Other contributors, such as Kingsley Amis and Iris Murdoch, were also one-time Labour supporters. Later Black Papers brought contributions from former progressive teachers – the Liberal Renee Soskin and the Froebel-trained Dolly Walker, who had exposed the iniquities of progressive education at William Tyndale Junior School in Islington. Equally important was the accessibility of the Papers: short essays – humorous, critical, nostalgic, that evoked enduring but presently neglected values. The range of voices was also important: probation officers alongside Cambridge dons; primary teachers next to literary celebrities. In both tone and range, the Papers had the advantage over many of their critics, whose responses, couched in the language of educationists or Labour politicians, seemed to lack vividness, informed personal conviction, and the ability to recognize and reflect on the problems of reform. They established a pamphleteering tradition which was to serve the right well.

As early as 1971, the Black Papers claimed to have 'broken the fashionable left-wing consensus' on education. Certainly, they had challenged it, but there followed plenty of evidence that they had not arrested the growth of the attitudes and policies

41

they condemned. Under the Conservative government of Edward Heath, the pace of comprehensivization increased. Mrs Thatcher, as Education Secretary, according to the Tory journalist Ronald Butt, 'was a good deal more cautious in challenging the orthodoxy than many of her party would have liked.' The Bullock Committee, set up by Mrs Thatcher to inquire into the teaching of English in schools – and thus to consider charges about declining standards of literacy – had reported in terms that did not break from the detested consensus, and that provoked a statement of dissent from its Black Paper member. In some areas, radical reforms of curriculum and internal school organization were introduced. Teachers, far from re-establishing themselves as the guardians of disinterested educational values, had struck for, and won, substantial pay increases. A revived Marxism had gained a foothold among teachers and students in higher education. All this took place, of course, against the background of a wider turbulence that, as we have seen, so frightened, and gave stimulus to, a resurgent right.

In this context, the Black Papers swerved to the right, giving up all hope for a moderation of Labour Party policy, and rethinking in greater detail their own programme after the stasis and disappointment of the Heath era. In 1975, the Conservative politician Rhodes Boyson became co-editor, alongside Brian Cox. That same year, in his book *Crisis in Education*, Boyson, earlier than other Conservatives, had given thought to the way that parental choice could be turned from a general principle to a basis for organization of the school system, and had also floated the idea of a national curriculum. Under his co-editorship, a second generation of contributors appeared – Caroline Cox, Edward Norman, Stuart Sexton – who were, or who became, much more closely involved with the right-wing of Conservative policy-making. Correspondingly, there was a marked re-allocation of blame for the crisis, and re-identification of the forces and programmes that could resolve it. The last of the Black Papers, in 1977, claimed that the crisis in teaching was pervasive, not merely local. There was a 'breakdown in teaching' and it was 'time the NUT stopped pretending otherwise'. The rot was no longer limited to the political and administrative levels, but had spread more generally: 'fanatical devotees of progressive education' retained 'too much power in schools and colleges'.

Since the teachers could no longer be trusted, it was time to develop a more elaborate programme for education. Of the earlier Black Paper programme, only the stress on selection was retained. No longer was the height of their ambition to limit the damage done by the extremism of Labour. Instead, a more confident and wide-ranging set of alternatives was advanced, that in many ways prefigured the Conservative policies of the 1980s. Children should be tested at the ages of 7, 11 and 14. Results should be published. There should be a 'core curriculum' of literacy, numeracy and a 'body of knowledge we should expect all our citizens to acquire'. Progressive educational methods should be confined to a small number of experimental schools. There should be an apprenticeship model of teacher training, to reduce the influence of theories that were fashionable in the academy but useless or harmful to the school. A voucher system 'or some other method' should be introduced, in order that parental choice could shape the education system. The direct grant (semi-independent) grammar schools should be re-absorbed into the state system, and used as super-selective academic schools to keep scholarship alive and show the standards possible with bright children. Conversely, 'schools that few wish to attend should be closed'.

In these ideas, developed out of the conferences organized by the National Council for Educational Standards, and made known to a wider audience by Stuart Sexton, the Black Papers linked their critique of educational standards (still essentially nostalgic) to free market ideas for restructuring education. This was a crucial juncture for the new right: a policy synthesis in which parents had a central role in determining the quality as well as the organizational outline of education.

There was also, now, a difference in the way that the Black Papers presented the theme of cultural crisis. Earlier contributions had written of it in terms which owed much to a tradition of 'culture-criticism' that regretted the effects of modernity, commercialism and industrial society on morality, standards and the quality of life. Embedded within this presentation were, of course, specific criticisms of the institutions and forces that, within education, had contributed to this decline. But there was no systematic attempt to politicize the analysis, in the sense of theorizing Labour's educational policy as evidence of some grander strategy for the destruction of society. Likewise, the earlier papers did not feel it necessary to call into being a militant, mobilized counter-reformation. Moderation would be appealed to, as a means of tempering the extremism of reform. The 1977 Black Paper took a different line. Just as the new leadership of the Conservative Party under Margaret Thatcher had begun to elaborate the themes of a strategy to transform the political institutions and the social values that had grown up around the post-war settlement, so the Black Paper began to develop a more politicized and wider-reaching critique of reform, and to devise a rhetoric of mobilization to bring about its overthrow. The 1977 Paper contained a section entitled 'Values'. In it, a figure of some importance in the revival of Conservative cultural theory published an essay on religious education. Edward Norman, Dean of Peterhouse College Cambridge, argued that changes in religious education – a subject he would prefer to rename 'Instruction' – had weakened both its Christian content and the school's ability authoritatively to transmit the culture of Britain. Instruction had become exploration; values had been relativized; liberals were claiming that England had become a 'pluralist' society. All of these developments were opposed by Norman – the last with especial vehemence. It was here that the novelty of the article lay: earlier contributors had talked of a breakdown in cultural transmission, but Norman was the first to relate the breakdown to a general ideological trend within the intelligentsia, and to set it within stringently national terms. 'England', he asserted, 'is not a pluralist society except in the most qualified sense. It is, on the contrary, a society whose leaders of opinion have lost confidence in their own traditional values and who represent the resulting chaos as reasoned diversity.' 'Nations of high morale and with confidence in their own values' would never have behaved in this way. Amid the railing against intellectuals who 'put the inherited values of their society up for sale', there was, though, a certainty that the beliefs and attitudes still survived on which this *trahison des clercs* would founder. Working-class and lower middle class society 'show few signs of religious or moral diversity'. They could form a basis of support for the fostering of 'solid' and 'decent' values. It was here that there existed a place for Christian instruction. Christianity thus served, independently of its theological content, as an expression of a single, unified moral tradition around which opposition to pluralism could cluster.

For much of its length, the target of Norman's essay was liberal pluralism. It concluded, though, with a warning that took his argument further, to a new level of danger: if the course of relativism was pursued, and if traditional values continued to be called into question, then the ultimate beneficiaries would be 'the hard men of ideology', who were already in the wings, awaiting their turn. The alternative to Norman's authoritarianism was not, in the last analysis, liberalism, but Marxism. Another article in the 'Values' section made the same case. Two of its three authors were John Marks and Caroline Cox, both of whom later rose to prominence on the educational right. Marxism, they said, was ascendant in the universities and polytechnics, and posed a threat to academic values more deadly even than the student unrest of earlier years. Marxism (like Norman perhaps) despised the bourgeois qualities of 'pluralism and tolerance'. It regarded the writings of Marx and his 'revered followers' as authoritative and Marxist analysis as infallible. Its politics were manipulative and intimidatory. As a sketch of Marxism in the 1970s, which far from being a secular monotheism was in fact teeming with schisms and revisionism, the article was luridly inaccurate. More important than its accuracy, though, was the part it played in raising the political stakes for which the right were fighting. Now the enemy was no longer simply the foolishness of Labour politicians and the complacent experimentation of educators, but rather an alien totalitarianism which was gathering force and menace.

On from the Black Papers 1: the free market

The last of the Black Papers, then, pointed in two directions. One pressed along the familiar track of concern for education's role in the preservation of standards and values. This track was soon to broaden as it joined new lines of right-wing political theory, in ways prefigured by Norman's article. Before 1977, the educational concerns of the right had merely implied a range of issues. Increasingly,afterwards, implication was replaced by an explicit linking. What happened in education was interpreted in terms that reflected the importance of culture, authority and nation in the programme of the right.

The second direction was that indicated in Stuart Sexton's article. The right moved from rearguard action against the advance of egalitarian reform to the beginnings of an offensive against it, whose aim would be its replacement by a different social and economic order. Crucial to this work was the growth of corporately funded think tanks and pressure groups. Generous subsidy from business made the Centre for Policy Studies, Keith Joseph's 1974 brainchild, the most prolific of these institutions. With donations from the Hanson Trust conglomerate, Kelloggs, Glaxo, Beechams and GKN, and with industrialists from Bass, British Steel and Gestetner on its board, the CPS experienced no financial difficulties in pursuing its aim of 'improving the standard of living, quality of life and freedom policies'. Likewise, the Social Affairs Unit, whose parent body, the free market supporting Institute of Economic Affairs, received nearly £500,000 in corporate donations. The Adam Smith Institute, a more modest enterprise, was less well-funded but, as we shall see, was hardly lacking in influence. These bodies, in the early and middle years of the Thatcher administration, all produced polemics and programmes of a more detailed and systematic type than the Black Papers had managed. While often less populist in their approach, they were able to build on the success of their predecessor and make closer links with the policy-making process. It is to their efforts that this chapter now turns, in setting out the most systematic and influential work of the free market right, that culminated in the Adam Smith Institute's *Omega File* of 1983/4.

The Black Papers were not without their comments on the unaccountability of those who controlled and worked in education. These observations, however, did not amount to any general theory, any 'law of bureaucracy'. Under the impact of free market thought such a theory, in the early 1980s was brought to bear on the education system: the indifference of the educational establishment to what was thought of as popular demand was not an accident; it followed inexorably from the nature of a system which had been removed from the pressures of the market-place, to be 'put under political direction and control'. Education was one of the great state monopolies, with its 'army of bureaucrats' imposing policies from on high, that resulted in 'shabby and outdated services'.

The educational consequences of intrinsically unaccountable monopoly control were many and serious. Operating on an assured income, schools were 'complacent about existing practices'; they 'failed to innovate' in any constructive sense, while at the same time were all too susceptible to the political whims of teachers, some of whom found it 'easier to spout their political prejudices to their charges than to make the intellectual effort to master a real subject, let alone to teach it'. Not needing to be receptive to consumer influence, schools had developed 'an educational bias against the business community', while themselves being, in economic terms, highly inefficient institutions. Top heavy with administrators, overstaffed with teachers, the school system had failed to respond effectively to the 'new market conditions' created by falling rolls It could not regenerate itself, since, with the best will in the world, teachers still could not escape the pressures of a monopoly situation.

'However dedicated they may be as educators, however concerned they may be as parents, the cocoon of producer interest keeps spinning round them. Their working environment wears each one down until they firmly accept that teachers deserve more money, should not be expected to supervise school meals, need smaller classes, cannot teach properly without a degree, should not be judged by their examination results, should have a guaranteed job for life and so on.'

The solution to this set of chronic problems lay, of course, in the market. It was time to let the future of the system be decided not by politics, but by the 'wishes of consumers'. For some time, though, there was uncertainty on the right about the organizational form in which these wishes could be given their most powerful effect. Some argued for a voucher system, with local authority funding of schools being replaced by the award of grants – education vouchers – to parents, who, topping them up if they desired, would cash them in for their child's education at a school of their choice. The problem with this scheme was political; it would be an all-or-nothing attempt to transform education that would instantly 'unify the educational establishment against it'. Thus the idea, though floated at the time of the 1983 election, was discarded as a practical alternative to the present system. There were other, subtler and more productive ways of exposing the school to the disciplines of the market. Responsibility for the running of schools should be devolved to school level, where it would become the property of 'school boards' dominated by parents. The LEA's role would be confined to the channeling of funds – largely provided by central government – to schools. The size of the funding would depend on the number of students a school attracted. By responding to market demand, schools could increase their intake and their income. 'Wrong decisions would be reflected in falling school rolls.' The school boards would thus be presiding over enterprises, where competitive efficiency would be at a premium. Competitiveness could be enhanced in a number of ways. Schools could cut their costs by improving the productivity of their staff. Teachers' security of tenure, and the protection of their conditions and pay through collective agreements, would be ended. Each teacher would be placed on an individual contract, with his or her work assessed annually. Qualified teacher status – another monopolistic shibboleth – would become less important, and teachers could be trained more cheaply and over shorter periods. 'Outsiders' with relevant experience – gained in industry, perhaps – should be employed. The headteacher would be free to arrange cooking and cleaning for the smallest possible cost, perhaps by using volunteer parent labour. Additionally, the schools would be encouraged to seek other sources of finance, perhaps through tax deductible gifts from parents and the business community.

The influence of the state in this gigantic new enterprise zone would no longer be pervasive; it would be concentrated at a few key points, to secure basic standards and to control subversion. National guidelines would be laid down for a compulsory core of subjects. 'Fringe' and 'contentious' subjects could be made voluntary, so as to allow parents to remove their children from unwanted discussions of sex and politics. In relation to the core of subjects a new legal 'duty of balance' would be established: teaching in state schools should not be distinctive of any particular persuasion, nor should it be based on an analysis distinctive of any particular political ideology.

In these ways, the entire dynamic of the system would be changed, and, along with it, the views of all those involved in education. The most obvious immediate effect would be on teachers: the educators would either submit to their re-education by market principles, or face a loss of livelihood. But the system also entailed a substantial recasting of the role of parents. In the schools of the pre-Omega period, parents, across a local authority, shared a fairly similar experience – a rough common equivalence of provision, and curricular outlook. Because this experience was common, it was possible for parents, on particular occasions, to unite in demands for more resources or in defence of equality of treatment, against attempts to restore or extend selection. In the early and middle 1980s, some parents had shown a tendency to act in this collective way. Thousands, for instance, had campaigned to defend the ILEA against repeated threats of abolition. In Solihull, they had organised to prevent the re-introduction of grammar schools. In the London Borough of Redbridge, they had opposed the strengthening of selection. In the neighbouring (Labour) Borough of Barking and Dagenham, a prolonged strike by teachers against cuts had gained solid parental support. The power of such collective opinion was one reason why Conservative attempts to restore or extend grammar school provision had been so cautious, limited and unsuccessful, and also helped explain the continuous pressure that Conservative governments experienced on questions of educational spending.

There remained, then, a parental constituency wedded to ideas of universal provision and equality of treatment – and, incidentally, quite willing to make common cause with teachers in campaigning to secure it. The Omega proposals, quite as much as they were aimed at teachers and LEAs, were aimed at breaking up this constituency and the alliances it tended to form, so that instead of having a single interest in securing higher and equitable levels of provision, it would develop fragmented, sectional interests. Omega, again prefiguring later Conservative efforts, approached this task in a number of ways. The first operated at the level of definition. It was denied that parents shared a common interest with teachers. Listing the beliefs of teachers on matters of class size, working conditions and pay, the report claimed that 'such arguments never emerge from the parents they are supposed to be serving'. Rather than being in any sense allies of teachers, parents were encouraged to think of themselves as among the *consumers* of education, whose interests were separated from those of the teacher-producers by an immense and widening gulf. Along with this language of division went an effort, widespread in Conservative thought as a whole, to fix the meaning of the term 'consumer'. It was reloaded with what Hilary Wainwright has called 'positive connotations of variety, choice and self-respect', and distinguished from the 'standardized' and passive client of the welfare state.

The second type of parental re-education was of a more practical kind. The Omega system would set parents off on a search for opportunity, that wondrous 'escape from disadvantages of birth' denied them by 'those social engineers who wish to prevent the dynamism of diversity'. This search would involve whole families, as they 'faced up to their new responsibilities' and 'discussed and decided on educational matters'. Having made their choice, their particular human investment in a school, they could then increase its value by their own further commitment – by seeking funds for the school, by taking part in its management, by working in its kitchens, helping it to form business links, and by whatever other devoted means became available. To this they could add an extra vigilance, against the potential derelictions of the producers. Turned towards these interests, they would forsake their previous roles. In these ways, Omega proposed an extensive wholescale reshaping of consciousness that would be all the more powerful for depending not on political conversion, but on the pressures of market forces. Imperceptibly, the interests and outlook of parents would be re-formed, as they went about the daily, undramatic but ceaseless business of working the system to their families' best advantage.

Such, at least, was the theory. Its attractions for the new right are evident; whether it is a stable basis for a permanent 'conservatization' of educational interest is an issue which will be discussed later. At this point, it is enough to note only its insufficiency as a political programme. Essentially, it was a blueprint for a future system. It did not have a close relationship to the major issues of education, as they were presented in public debate and campaigning. It did not reflect the demands of any section of educational opinion – councils, parents, students or teachers. Nor could it muster a particularly inspiring ideology of educational purpose, that related to deeply-felt identities and desires. Efforts to provide it with an affective dimension rang somewhat feebly. Either they expressed consumer ideology in the most banal of ways – as in the demand of one MP that education should aspire to the condition of Marks and Spencer in 'guaranteeing a choice of quality goods served by well-trained staff in a disciplined environment under the supervision of strong management'; or else they tended to an implausible idealization of the market. 'The unthinking deride the free market', read one pamphlet of the right, 'as if it were some kind of sordid commercial transaction which reduces everything to buying and selling. They miss the central truth that the market is about human values and relationships. It is by choosing to spend more on such things as health care that a person expresses a say on the subject. It is by doing so that he or she achieves input to the system, instead of being a passive recipient of someone else's priorities.'

These market place ideals cut little ice. To make a political impact, some other cause was needed, that had a less cavalier attitude to ideas of a common interest in welfare provision, a closer relationship to popular desires and discontents, and a correspondingly greater agitational capacity. Explaining the causes of his own success, Richard Vigurie, the direct mail wizard of the American new right, noted that,

'It was the social issues that got us this far .... We never really won until we began stressing issues like bussing, abortion, school prayer and gun control. We talked about the sanctity of free enterprise, about the Communist onslaught until we were blue in the face. But we didn't start winning majorities in elections until we got down to the gut level issues.'

For the English right, the gut level issues were those set out by the Dean of Peterhouse. In the formation of a political strategy, the line of thought represented by Norman's article took on a special value. Culture, authority, nation and – increasingly –

51

race became the dynamic themes of the Conservative politics of education.

On from the Black Papers 2: culture and race

Culture is, of course, a term capable of almost infinite variety of meaning. In the particular inflections that the right gives it, it concerns:

a way of life constructed on a national basis, out of national traditions;

an integrative set of meanings and interpretations: culture binds a nation together;

the 'essential identity' of individuals. Culture, as Roger Scruton puts it, 'affirms one's reality as a social being'. It reaches to the core of an individual's existence and determines their deepest affiliations.

The gap between these understandings of 'culture' and others current on the official educational scene needs to be registered. It shares few points of connection with the 'culture of enterprise' or 'culture of technology' that modernizers in the Conservative Party would like to see evolve. Its interests lie away from 'technik', in areas of language, history and tradition, and in this it shares in all the hegemonic themes of British intellectual life so detested by some of those who seek industrial regeneration. Yet, economically obstructive though they may be, these themes are ideologically potent. Some are relatively timeless: they register, from a particular angle, the changes and dislocations inherent in modern capitalism. The lament for the standards and the discipline which once, it is suggested, organized a culture around a clear and authoritative body of knowledge, crystallizes discontent with the conflicts and complexities of modern education. Such bitter nostalgia contributed to the appeal of the Black Papers, and has by no means disappeared since. Yet it is evident that the mobilizing power of the right in education is stronger than it was a decade ago, and has a new fervour and effectiveness. Nostalgia alone is not the driving force of this advance, to understand which we have to look beyond protest against change in education, towards some central issues in the national culture of Mrs Thatcher's England.

The results of the coincidence of economic decline, the break-up of the culture and industry of the cities, and mass immigration from ex-colonial countries have been too often noted to need elaborating here. For my purposes, one single theme needs picking out: *race* has provided a vocabulary in which right-wing intellectuals and politicians can speak to the 'nation' about what it is, and what is happening to it, and through the medium of race they can interpret some of the central experiences of the times. Immigration, in the 1960s, offered the first opportunity for such interpretation, and it was Enoch Powell who took it. Through Powell, as Tom Nairn wrote, it 'became possible to define Englishness vis a vis this "internal enemy" ' – the immigrant – 'this foreign body in our own streets'. The reverberations of this linking, this conjuring of identity through the naming of its opposite, run through the right's subsequent treatment of cultural themes. Around it clustered other concerns, many of them expressing in direct or indirect ways real problems at the base of British society: complaints about bureaucracy; demands for choice, not state direction; threnodies for the loss of 'community spirit', and so on. In the early 1980s Powell could again attempt to evoke an ancestral patriality, in denouncing state policies that aimed to integrate 'immigrants' within an avowedly pluralist society. He called up a vision of an Englishness 'rooted in its homeland ... continuous with its past', opposed to bureaucratically-led attempts to 'force upon ourselves a non-identity and to assert that we have no unique distinguishing characteristics: the formula is a "multi-racial, multi-cultural society" ' Powell here discussed multi-culturalism, that mildest of responses to 'race issues', in terms of the annihilation of identity: hyperbole is the currency of the right's treatment of race. More radical measures against racism met with a yet more inflated – and calculating – response. Anti-racism, argued a Monday Club pamphlet, was 'an indictment of a people, the white British, and their way of life'. Positive action for the employment of blacks was a 'reverse racism' that overturned traditional British ideas of fairness. Anti-racism in schools demanded that the indigenous population re-evaluated its own past, and required it 'to accept

53

major changes in its own way of life'. Worse, it contributed towards transforming schools into political, not educational, institutions, that would promote a 'cynical if not openly hostile outlook on British society and all major British institutions, including forces of law and order'.

Race, then, stands at the heart of a discourse that organizes the interpretation of a wide range of experience. The next two sections examine the interplay of questions of culture and education with those of nation and race in the work of two of the most effective intellectuals of the right: the journalist and professor of aesthetics, Roger Scruton and the local councillor and former primary headteacher Ray Honeyford. They belong to a committed and activist intelligentsia that has done much to develop a Conservative education programme, and to find those points of intervention into everyday life that can give it a popular appeal. As a whole, this intelligentsia is neither in origin nor in orientation part of a traditional Tory elite. For the most part grammar school educated, based outside the old universities, or in the school sector, often of one time sympathy for the Labour Party, it is a new force in Conservative intellectual politics.

These activists are critical of previous right-wing responses to social-democratic reform. As Honeyford puts it, they 'failed to take state education seriously', either through over-concern with the private sector or through accommodation to ideologies of equal opportunity, even though 'there were no rationally defensible educational findings' to justify comprehensive schooling. 'Socialist and marxist intellectuals' on the other hand, have 'had direct and precise effects on actual policy formation at both local and national levels.' Honeyford wants the right to learn from such achievements even while it overthrows them, and it is this duality of response – the desire to emulate mixed with the intention to destroy – that makes his politics, like that of other right-wingers, truly counter-reformational. Like Honeyford, and in a more committed way than recent generations of socialists, the new right has been concerned to educate, to agitate and organize. It has been attentive to popular grievance, which it has reformulated in the language of race. It has produced attempts, at least, at academic research into the standards question. It has set up publishing houses. It has used the media to popularize its ideas. It has encouraged

Conservative LEAs, such as Berkshire, to develop policy on race that overturns established and consensual priorities, and worked to hold in check the initiatives of Labour authorities, such as Brent. It has intervened in particular controversies, to give its intuitive supporters assistance and to generalize their experience. (Thus the white parents in Dewsbury, West Yorkshire, who did not wish their children to attend a predominantly Asian school were assisted by the 'Parental Alliance for Choice in Education', and those white mothers in Manchester who did not want their children to experience multi-cultural religious education, were funded in their legal action by the Freedom Association.)

Roger Scruton has been involved in many of these enterprises. In important ways, his intellectual work is activist and collaborative; it embraces not only academic study and publication, but prolific journalism and pamphleteering, as part of a programme of intervention in the politics of culture. He has a record of collective work on pamphlets and book-length projects, of accurate polemic and effective lobbying. He used his editorship of the *Salisbury Review* not just to develop a Conservative cultural philosophy, but also to bring into public intellectual life dissenting figures from the heartlands of educational reform. Having solicited their contributions to the review, he then, from his column in *The Times*, defended their views in terms which stirred further controversy.

For all his brilliance of style and relatively esoteric specialism (it is difficult to imagine Norman Tebbit approving of aesthetics) Scruton gives the impression of someone unusually close to the intuitions, prejudices, instinctive reactions and deep beliefs of his constituency, often to the point of sharing its silliness, ignorance and intemperance of judgement: a role that is very different from the dominant image of the twentieth-century intellectual. In other ways, too, Scruton seems a writer at ease in a particular version of English and European culture, who moves without difficulty between 'high' culture and the popular: essays on Hayek and Wagner sit comfortably in his work alongside pieces in praise of popular dance and of the motor cycle. The attitude is of a writer pointing out and expressing well what many will have noticed without articulation. One effect of the breadth of his interests is to validate his claim that cultural knowledge is 'inner knowledge' – that a culture only reveals its meanings to those who have experienced its nuances, habits and varieties. Perhaps written into his celebration of the culture is a tacit denial that its meanings will ever be available to those who hold back their full commitment from it: a refutation of the position taken up by other cultural analysts – Barthes, say, in *Mythologies*.

Scruton, in this aspect, is at home in his culture: the opposite of an outsider. He has an insider's influence, too. He has affected Conservative education policy in important ways, and his ideas in popular form have become the nostrums of such as the *Daily Mail*. Yet he claims to be writing from the fringes of intellectual life, against the dominant commonplaces. A leading intellectual, whose ideas find an echo in much Conservative social policy, lays explicit claim to the status of the outcast and the intellectual refugee. Why?

The first and most obvious reason is that Scruton, like many intellectuals of the right, places himself in opposition, not only to socialism, but to many tendencies that, deriving from the development of modern capitalism, sweep away the culture and the institutions which nourished his ideas. In addition, the particular sector – education – in which he has been most active is one whose official ideology remains influenced by reformist or progressive ideas. It is a sector in which there remains some small and diminishing space for radical experiment, within a consensus which continues to lie outside the boundaries of modern Conservatism. Within that sector, Scruton's voice may sound like the bitter and lonely call of a prophet, even though in the social order as a whole he may speak from a securer viewpoint. To this extent, his rage against the fashionable reflects the frustration of a political tendency which however much it is able to command the political arena has not yet imposed a decisive stamp on many areas of intellectual life. But there is also a more compelling reason for Scruton's stand: the need to clothe the dominant ideas in the garments of the virtuous oppressed – to wear the mantle of a fighter for justice and truth, in rebellion against the corruptions and inhumanities of the status quo. Just as the working-class autodidacts of the 1920s compiled collections that displayed the bias and capitalist ethic of schoolbooks and examination questions, so Scruton and his collaborators cut out and display evidence of what they take to be the new orthodoxy of anti-racism in mathematics, or of support for gay and lesbian rights in the policy statements of LEAs. Taking up a position like this is the right's most powerful rhetorical device; Scruton, and Honeyford, deploy it brilliantly.

How, then, do these attitudes relate to questions of race and nation? Scruton's view of culture is of a spontaneous order, the result over centuries of a myriad exchanges between individuals. The model is an organic one. It is notably free from consideration of the way that inequalities of power, access and opportunity have shaped cultures, and pays little attention to the conflicts over meaning that occur between social groups, and that are reproduced in individual actions and consciousness. 'Culture' is a profoundly unifying relationship – a sharing of meaning. While he would agree with Marxism that the sense that individuals make of the world is saturated by the understandings made available to them by their culture, his emphasis is on the unity, not the conflictual diversity, of cultural meanings. The consequence of this position is that conflicts over meaning are ascribed to differences *between* cultures, that are considered as separate, monolithic entities: there is a tendency to classify some meanings as alien intrusions into a culture, and as interruptions of cultural transmission.

The knowledge acquired through a culture is a form of 'practical knowledge'. It 'consists in knowing the appropriate responses, the inner meanings and the human content of a variety of given artefacts and institutions'. In England it involves 'an instruction in the nature of, and the feeling for, the English law: in the *Rechtsgefühl* (the feeling for law and justice) of England, upon which the 'English peace' is ultimately founded'. This is a feeling formed through appreciation of inequality, and through a certain kind of submission; it involves 'an ability to orientate one's outlook in the light of observations and emotions expressed by greater and more perceptive minds than oneself'. The transmission of culture also involves a more explicitly authoritative element, that centres on 'instruction'. In the context of English culture, this instruction is bound explicitly to particular notions of the rule of law that have served as the legitimizing foundation of the British state. In connecting culture so closely and fundamentally to the rule of law,

Scruton's model of culture would appear to be a politicized one. Yet it is also one of his major contentions that some of the most important things to be said about education in a cultural context concern its non-programmatic character. He criticizes radicals who 'have a natural tendency to see every question, every decision and every institution in political terms: that is, as the expression of a particular set of political values and therefore as a pre-empting of every political position except one'. For him, education as traditionally conceived 'can have no programme'. It emerges from the free flow of interests, not from some pre-set list of priorities. Alternative, politicized approaches are based not on open-minded investigation but on 'foregone conclusions'. In a 'flood of vociferating ignorance' they destroy the patient work of scholars across centuries who have built up and defined the traditional bodies of knowledge and fields of study.

The paradox of the argument is evident. While claiming for his own commitment to the rule of law and to other traditions associated with the British political order a supra-political status, he damns with the 'political' label those who seek to redefine or reselect the leading elements of culture, and charges them with a work of intellectual ruination. The political advantages of the position are likewise plain. The left can be presented as an intrusive and barbarizing element, that reduces all questions to ones of politics, and seeks everywhere for 'relations of power' where others will find only natural 'differences of endowment'.

Of all educational developments, it is anti-racism which provokes Scruton to his most furious defence of educational value and British culture. Anti-racism is a major target of the pamphlets he helped produce for the Hillgate Group, and of *Education and Indoctrination*, on which he collaborated in 1985; it is a frequent topic in his journalism and the subject of an entire book edited by his protege Frank Palmer, to which Scruton contributed. It perhaps provokes his fury because of all radical contributions to the educational debate it is the most alert to the shaping of British and European culture by imperialisms past and present. Every document of civilization, wrote Walter Benjamin, is also a document of barbarism; and it is the 'barbaric' side of European culture on which anti-racism has shone its light. Demanding a re-evaluation of an entire history, it has also called into question biases, silences and discrimination that are woven into the fabric of British schooling. Where Scruton finds freedom under the law, in a unified culture, anti-racism would discover conflict and oppression; in those places from which he expels politics, anti-racism would call it back in.

The alternative readings that anti-racism suggests are for Scruton profoundly disturbing of British identity, and of education's claim to be based on values other than the political. His reaction to them is extremely sharp. How dare the anti-racists find in the public school of the nineteenth century an agency that inculcated 'the values and norms of colonial and imperial Britain'. How crass to assert that the century was one which saw 'racism as an ideology institutionalised' in British society. How foolish to try to 'invent a multi-cultural history' for Britain. And what ignorance of human nature to assume that xenophobia is not intrinsic to it, or to believe that ethnic minorities are any less racist than the culture in which they have settled.

But these are not merely errors of assessment or interpretation. They are signs of a more fundamental flaw. They run so much against the grain of what education is, that no 'educated person' could hold them. They must therefore be the views of the uneducated, whose 'virulent hostility and prejudice' towards the educated person set them apart from British culture. Their views represent at best the undermining, through a levelling multiculturalism, of a great tradition. At worst, they represent a totalitarian interest, that is hostile to educational autonomy and that seeks

> 'to gain control of important autonomous institutions where inconvenient truths may be uttered and where influence other than its own may flourish. To anyone who has studied the rise of totalitarian movements it will come as no surprise to find that the anti-racists wish to control local government and schools, two crucial centres through which power may be exercised not over the state but over something which for the totalitarian mind is far more important: civil society.'

The political methods of the anti-racists – their challenge to the traditions of a disinterested education – show, even more plainly than the substance of their interpretations of history and present-day society, by how much they have exceeded the limits of civilized debate, and the extent to which they have forfeited the privileges of toleration. Against such opponents, the most purposeful action, the sharpest legislation is necessary. And so Roger Scruton, the beleaguered oppositionist, the defender of the civilized virtues of intellectual debate, becomes Scruton the avenger, capable of triggering the most illiberal and intemperate legislation, and of encouraging the most inflamed and prejudiced of popular responses.

Scruton found his most celebrated cause in the controversy surrounding Ray Honeyford, head of a Bradford primary school, most of whose children came from 'Asian' families. In this role, Honeyford was concerned that their 'language problems' held back the progress of white English children and that Asian and West Indian parents showed no interest in coming to terms with the habits and attitudes demanded by an English education.

In the summer of 1983, Honeyford had published in *The Times Educational Supplement* a headteacher's diary, that described the problems as he saw them. In this piece the tone is fairly dispassionate, evoking the patience and resolution of the dedicated professional as he deals with the problems laid before him by the new cultures of the inner city. In the following year, he published another piece, this time in the *Salisbury Review*, which depicted the fury of a headteacher, driven to protest by the resistance of 'Asian communities' and educational bureaucracies to the simple and reasonable policies for which he sought support. This article started from an account of particular experiences, and went on to make some general comments about the relationship of Asian and black families to English schools. The article led to calls for his dismissal by parents at the school and to suggestions by the local NUT branch that he should cease to be the school's headteacher. The campaign thus initiated lasted for the next eighteen months and eventually led to Honeyford's retirement, with compensation. During that time, he again published in the *Salisbury Review* and was defended by Scruton in *The Times*. His name was chanted at football matches, as a rallying call for racism. Honeyford himself, a hero in the popular press, was received at Downing Street, and now appears to be a well-integrated member of the educational right, a Conservative local councillor – elected in 1988 – with an increasing list of publications to his name.

The Honeyford case was far more than an intellectual dispute, or an issue fought out within a limited educational arena. It was, from its earliest days, a *popular* issue, that was manifested on the street and in communities, and not solely within schools, education offices and union meetings. It was also a test case, to determine the success of the new right's education programme; did the issues it identified have a real life at the base of society? Could they be presented as a fundamental conflict between freedom and oppression, truth and its suppression? Could the case of Honeyford be used further to weaken the cause of educational reform? The opportunity was promising. In Honeyford, the right had found a talented writer, well worth the care and encouragement that Scruton gave him. Working class in social origin, formerly a Labour supporter, he was another who possessed the credentials to speak with an authentic, experience-born disillusion about the consequences that followed the pursuit of equal opportunity and cultural diversity. Similarly, his role of busy and committed head teacher allowed him to claim a further authenticity for his views. 'Experience' and 'truthfulness' are the hallmarks of a rhetoric that Honeyford employs to great effect.

It is Honeyford's view that there exists a 'perpetual war between reason and dogma'. He clearly regards himself as a soldier of reason, who faces unflinchingly the reality of a situation and speaks the truth about it. His first *Salisbury Review* article, the one that began the controversy, refers to the 'raw feel of reality' which he wishes to communicate. But it is difficult, he claims, to do this, since the very language in which to identify situations and to voice experiences has been stifled by tyranny. Like Milovan Djilas, says Honeyford, he intends to challenge the way that despots (in this context, 'the growing bureaucracy of race') 'have perverted language to sustain their ideology'. The entire debate about race and education has been conducted 'in a language which is dishonest'. Nevertheless, he intends to 'make a start' towards 'inventing' a language by commenting on his 'everyday experiences'. In doing so, he will articulate the intuitions of 'decent people uncertain of their right to think certain thoughts', seeking a language 'by means of which doubts, fears and aspirations can be expressed openly and honestly'.

Thus Honeyford proceeds by a route that mimics the struggles over meaning and language conducted by oppressed groups: it is a matter of finding a voice in which to speak the truth against the vast and 'intimidating' mendacity of the established order. (Like Scruton, Honeyford finds many advantages in claiming as his own the position of the dispossessed.)

What then is the reality of which he proposes to speak? It is not the reality of racism, since that is something he barely recognizes. He does not accept the claim of institutional racism in employment for instance, because 'variations in ethnic representation in various jobs are to be expected in societies which are both free and multi-cultural'. Besides, he has found that although natural xenophobia makes most people pre-judiced, this leads neither to racism (defined as a 'doctrine of racial superiority') nor to discrimination. Most people in Britain are 'prejudiced non-discriminators'. No – the reality of which he intends to speak is that of the 'plight of those white children who constitute the 'ethnic minority' in a growing number of inner city schools', and of the insensitivity of immigrant groups to their own status within a host culture. These are the experiences for which Honeyford wishes to find a language – one that can affect the perception and the definition of reality.

Problems of language and of conceptualization are central to the article, which seeks less to set out a policy than to find a voice. In fact, when found, the voice turns out to be a familiar one, which communicates in its vocabulary and inflections a hostility and contempt towards the 'immigrant' population. Its rhetoric of insult works in a number of ways. First, it refuses to adopt the terms that black and Asian people use to describe themselves. Honeyford speaks of 'brown parents' and of 'negroes'. Second, it is brazenly stereotypical, speaking with sarcasm of 'the West Indian's right to create an ear-splitting cacophony' or of Muslim parents 'imposing a purdah mentality'. Then it counterposes to the irrationality of the East the simple and straightforward nature of the English system. 'Asian immigrants' who 'have a habit' of sending their children to India or Pakistan on holiday have to have 'explained' to them 'the importance of regular school attendance for their offspring's future'. Honeyford, in fact, called a meeting to do precisely this. Whereupon, 'the hysterical political temperament of the Indian sub-continent became evident, an extraordinary sight in an English school hall'. The Asians 'wildly and implacably resented ... the simple British requirement on all parents to send their children to school regularly'.

So, far from struggling like a poet to invent a new language adequate to experience, Honeyford triggers with great facility a familiar variety of hostilities towards ethnic minority parents. The craft, or craftiness, of the rhetoric lies in its deniability Honeyford, unless he possesses an uncommon ignorance of everyday life, must know that his comments establish a relationship with a whole discourse of racism. They relate to claims about black aggression, irrationality, ignorance, insensitivity, privilege – and most fundamentally of all to the claim that the presence of blacks is a factor that holds back the achievement of white children. Nevertheless, because the racism lies less in the argument of the article than in the connections its language establishes with other discourses, and because the counterposition of British sense with Asian insensitivity is established by means of art rather than assertion, he is able to deflect attacks on his racism, and to claim for his article the brave status of a piece of truth-telling.

In *The Times* Scruton called Honeyford's incitement 'a seriously argued article, almost every word of which I believe to be true'. The crime of Mr Honeyford 'was to tell the truth as he saw it', written out of the harsh experience of 'one who must confront each day the fate of white working class children... whose equal opportunities are increasingly threatened.' (It did not bother Scruton that a few weeks previously he had referred to the high achievement of Asian students as a means of disposing of charges that the school system is racist.) The enemies of these white children are 'people who despise our traditions of understatement, civilised discourse and respect for truth'. By contrast Honeyford's article, 'brown parents' and all, displayed 'the natural instinct of the rational animal ... drew attention to the problems presented by multi-cultural education ... and presented, in British fashion, a sceptical conclusion. All of which is part of the spirit of compromise.'

Scruton's ability to discover qualities of rationality, scepticism and compromise in the incessant linguistic provocations of Honeyford's article calls into question his claims for the restraint and truthfulness of his own writing, as well as the nature of the values on which he takes his stand. Nevertheless, it also exemplifies one of the strengths of the right. It can combine in breath-taking ways a gutter invective with the claim to the all-but-lost traditions of high culture. It is difficult, of course, to measure the practical effect of this rhetoric, and of the political interventions to which it is bound, but one fact may nevertheless be salient. By 1988, of all the large northern cities, the only one of which the Conservatives were in political control – having recently defeated Labour – was Bradford.

On from the Black Papers 3: The model curriculum

Honeyford, and Scruton in his journalistic mode, could mobilize public opinion, but influence the implementation of educational policy only indirectly and in uncertain ways. To challenge the new orthodoxy most effectively, the right saw a need for something more – an attention to the detail of what happens in schools and the means whereby it is promoted and controlled. It needed a closer focus on teaching, learning, examining and inspecting – which all remained in the hands of an 'establishment' that still adhered to the orthodoxies of the 1960s. Lacking this, concluded John Marenbon, 'ministers of government, preoccupied with the external politics of education, have repeatedly been defeated in the more important internal politics of what is taught and how: defeated by an enemy they do not recognise, in a battle they do not know they are fighting'. Increasingly in the later 1980s, the right involved itself in these curriculum wars. For several reasons, its chosen battlefields were the teaching of English and of history. The kinds of understanding of culture prevalent on the right led it towards these areas, and it was there that its political project could most easily take hold, in developing themes of identity and nation. It was also the case that English and history were strongpoints of opposition, where radical ideas were deeply embedded. In other subjects, the right thought, political interference was easy to spot; it appeared as a rhetoric surrounding particular skills and competences, extrinsic to them, that on occasion interrupted in blatant ways their true content. Anti-racism in mathematics was a case in point. But, in English, the very definitions of the subject were those formulated by radical thinkers: though the intellectual legacy of F.R. Leavis was a deeply ambiguous one, he had established a dissenting, critical attitude to twentieth-century culture at the centre of 'English'; and, in the intellectual climate of the 1960s and 1970s, this radicalism had been deepened rather than forgotten. History in schools, with its relativistic methods and increasing bias towards the social and the economic reflected the work of Marxist and radical historians in creating what one critic called a 'shop steward syllabus' of modern history. There were dangers, too, of a more extreme politicization. Since the 1970s, English had been flooded by the 'dissemination of cultural values and attitudes associated with the most urgent social and political conflicts'. Similarly, 'the lack of serious discussion about heritage and tradition' in history created an 'ideological vacuum' into which flew 'a host of irrational and malignant sprites', such as the 'new racism [that] emerged in Britain in the early 1980s under the aegis of ILEA'. As a national curriculum became an increasingly likely outcome of state policy, so the strategic objective of the right became more focused: to ensure that what it called the 'consensus of the 1960s' played no part in formulating the courses of study and assessment targets integral to a national curriculum. The right's attack thus centred around the issue of progressive influence, rather than simply the more radical extremities of curriculum development.

Earlier writers had laid the basis for a critique of modern 'English', with its dislike for the teaching of grammar, vocabulary, expression and the other 'hard parts' of the subject, and of the hostility of progressive history to 'the notion of ever establishing any objective facts about the world'. In 1987-8, these lines of argument were developed and made systematic in a series of pamphlets published by the Centre for Policy Studies. The clearest overall statement of their case is made by Sheila Lawlor, who lists the fatal theses of the new orthodoxy:

'The theory is that there should be no absolute standards; that teaching is not a matter of passing on a body of knowledge; that what is taught must be relevant to the child's world; that practical and investigative work is as important as other work – as also is discussion and talking; that teaching should not be confined to narrow subjects but should be across the curriculum; that education has a 'social role'; and that learning should be promoted through games, puzzles and enjoyment'.

She dissents from these ideas at every point. Standards can be maintained only if they are clearly and publicly defined. Without learning a definite body of knowledge, pupils will 'flounder'. 'Relevance' is a false god; far better that a pupil 'master the principles' of a subject, so that whatever the problem 'he can apply them' to it. The emphasis on practical work has become an end in itself, instead of a means of acquiring knowledge. There is, she asserts, in defiance of half a century of research, 'no reason to imagine that pupils learn from talking'. The 'emphasis on cross-curricular teaching makes it difficult for pupils to acquire knowledge and techniques in any given area'. As for the social role of education, it is 'nothing more than a crude attempt at social conditioning', which 'should not be the task of any school'. Finally, learning cannot be attained through play, but only through 'hard and conscious effort'.

Lawlor's ideas form the intellectual framework for John Marenbon's pamphlet *English, Whose English?*. Marenbon, a Cambridge mediaevalist, is as detailed as Lawlor in outlining the tenets of a modern education, and their deficiencies. English teachers – among whom he includes exam boards and the school inspectorate – have rejected the idea of English as a subject that requires the imparting of a particular body of knowledge. In fact, they have abandoned the whole idea of teaching as knowledge-transmission altogether, in favour of a child-centred approach that values the spoken as much as the written, the local dialect as much as the national standard, and that refuses to set absolute standards of correctness in language, preferring a loose and intellectually disreputable criterion of 'appropriateness'. In as much as this establishment accepts the importance of the teaching of literature, it does so only in ways that utilize it as a springboard for 'imaginative and personal response' or as an occasion for practical criticism. In each case there is no concern to inculcate a knowledge of the literary tradition.

Marenbon's presentation, like Lawlor's, is full of wild overstatements, and displays a total lack of interest in the questions of how learning takes place that have so occupied the tradition he criticizes. Nevertheless, he is not without the elements of a case: there are unresolved issues and confusions in the teaching of English, and the role of Standard English is undoubtedly one of them. The question is, however, whether from his position it is possible to appreciate the inter-related issues of culture and intellectual development that lie at the heart of debates about Standard English. His alternative is plain enough. He wants to see English pursuing 'the simple and well-defined aims of teaching children to write and speak Standard English correctly, and of initiating their acquaintance with the literary heritage of the language'. To be able to use the standard form is a vital accomplishment. Most kinds of English are inadequate, by reason of grammar and syntax as well as vocabulary, to the task of 'presenting clearly a complicated, abstract argument'. A preference for Standard English is not a gratuitous snobbery, but is soundly based in history. The standard form is 'the language of English culture at its highest levels as it has developed over the last centuries: the language, not just of literature, philosophy and scholarship, but of government, science, commerce and industry'. Dialects of English, on the other hand, 'reflect the much more limited range of functions for which they have traditionally been used: the exchanges of everyday life, mainly among those unrefined by education'. Besides learning the standard forms of the language, students should come to know the literary masterpieces of the culture. In this way, they will come to acquire both that 'regard for literature [which] is itself a value' and the knowledge of the literary heritage which is an essential form of cultural understanding. The familiar emphases of progressive English are obstacles to this kind of education. The stress on oracy is redundant, since 'children learn to speak and listen just by being present at these activities'. The 'social role' of English is merely an intellectually unacceptable attempt to communicate a 'haphazard collection of virtues (maturity, tolerance and so on'). As for 'relevance', it should not dictate the content of the curriculum. 'A pupil's interest is merely a necessary condition for his learning: there is no good reason why it should determine what he learns.' What the pupil needs to know is established by the twin heritage of Standard English and the literary canon.

Far more than recommendations for the teaching of a single subject is contained in these ideas; they set out an entire philosophy of culture and pedagogy, whose premises require the closest examination. Fundamentally, Marenbon seeks to deny that true education is in any way connected with concerns that arise in any immediate sense from the lives of those who are involved in learning. This is the common thread of his arguments. It involves him in a process of erasing all signs that the content of education and the ways in which learning takes place have anything at all to do with class, or power, or any other social relationship but that between teacher and learner, which is determined by the unequal relation to knowledge that gives the teacher his or her ascendancy. Each of the two pillars of his English curriculum is scrubbed clean of the traces left by those who constructed it. Tradition and authority appear as impersonal, anonymous forces. This is most evidently the case in his treatment of the literary canon, even though it begins with what seems to be a startlingly relativist statement. 'Literary texts', he writes, 'are those texts ... which have come to be considered as literature.' Just for a moment, it seems as if Marenbon is going to allow that what counts as literature, let alone the literary canon, is affected by choices arising from recognizably social interests. However, the circular calm of cultural absolutism is soon restored; the relativism was only apparent. 'We learn what literature is, and how to read it by coming to read those works which are recognised as literature.' So, we learn what literature is from literature itself. To the convoluted, but at this stage necessary, question, 'How is it that the literature we read to find out what literature is, itself comes to be literature?' Marenbon takes refuge in a decorous passive. He speaks of works 'that have come to be considered as literature', or which 'are recognized' as such. Within that passive are hidden the mysteries of agency. Who has chosen, classified, considered and recognised some works, out of all the millions, as literature, and/or as part of the canon? On the basis of which criteria was the selection made? What ideas, with what social bases, shaped the criteria? What has been excluded, and why? The questions are not posed. As always with the new right, highly partisan and selective judgements about meaning and value pose as eternal absolutes, that need no justification, and that can serve as Olympian vantage-points from which to deride attempts to develop new courses of literary study, whose purposes and principles of selection are usually, and deliberately, left open for all to scrutinize and debate.

Marenbon's discussion of Standard English, his second pillar, is more substantial, and his contentions are important to any discussion of the relationship between language and conceptual development. He is right to argue that different languages and dialects possess, for historical reasons, qualitatively different possibilities of use. He is correct, too, in arguing that Standard English has these possibilities to a greater extent than other dialect forms. The problem comes from his failure to see the way that Standard English as a language of knowledge is interwoven with Standard English as a language of class. Not only in the accents of its speakers, or in its Latinate vocabulary, abstruse points of grammar and apparently more complex syntax, but in the forms of discourse in which non-standard users often encounter it, Standard English appears to many as a language that embodies particular powers or that conveys particular social attitudes. Yet the problems that its complex, combined nature poses for the classroom are not seen by Marenbon.

This failure is of a piece with his conception of the learning process. He lacks any conception of how what the American writer, Ira Shor, calls the 'paper rigour' of the right's curriculum can transfer itself into the conceptual and linguistic development of the student. He views education as an encounter between teachers, authoritative because of their access to a particular body of knowledge, and the uneducated student, whose role is to submit to the inexorable requirements of the subject. The fraught and *socially* difficult nature of learning is not appreciated, and so the difficulties that non-standard speakers might have with the standard form would be regarded only as evidence of an intellectual incapacity, or else of a wilful obstinacy. Questions of student rejection of what can be seen as an alienating or irrelevant form of language are not taken seriously. Correspondingly, the possibilities of other dialects as languages of learning are lost on him. Non-standard forms are for 'the exchanges of everyday life'. Their speakers, he admits, can be 'verbally agile within certain areas of discourse', and the topics traditionally discussed in the standard language are 'not entirely barred to them', but there is no recognition that understandings of the world, or complex conceptual developments can occur other than through the standard forms. His telling description of those who have not experienced the education familiar to him as the 'unrefined' is eloquent testimony to a huge failure of understanding and imagination: the cultures of working-class people, of ethnic minorities are closed books to him. The kinds of connection and interchange, sought by many teachers of English, between the intellectual resources of Standard English and the kinds of understanding that are expressed in more popular idiom are unthinkable. Pretending to be open to all and indifferent to particular interests, Marenbon's English, by presenting the achievements of the dominant culture as the timeless fruits of absolute standards of learning, endorses a curriculum and a pedagogy that involves the effective exclusion of great numbers of students from it. To accept his arguments about the nature and maintenance of standards is to collude with him in a project of restoring or defending inequalities.

A new orthodoxy is also the target of Alan Beattie's pamphlet on history teaching, *History in Peril: May Parents Preserve It*. It is responsible for placing history in peril, both through its addiction to particular principles of method and in its revision of the content of the subject. Like Marenbon, Beattie steps forward as a defender of classical disciplines against the anarchic relativism of curriculum reform. Under its influence, history in schools has degenerated from a factually-based body of knowledge to a method of inquiry-based learning that rejects the possibility of establishing the facts of any event. Students are encouraged not to acquire a solid grounding of historical information, but to go off on a facile search for 'bias' in the viewpoints of historians, to make anachronistic moral judgements about other times and to rely on empathy and imagination in re-creating the world of the past. In as much as this kind of 'history' has a stable content it is dominated by a mixture of events too recent to allow dispassionate and well-documented study, by histories outside the British story, and by economic and social themes; British political history is no longer taught. Few of these changes are the result of considerations relevant to history. Instead, they have been generated mainly by ideological developments within educational institutions, which have 'exceeded their authority' by reshaping 'what is taught as history ... in pursuit of wider social ends'. It is time for parents to redress the balance; the government should subject education to a rigorous regime of consumer choice, so that a healthier kind of history may be restored.

Like Marenbon, Beattie sets out his own, alternative ideas of the discipline very clearly. They are views which extend beyond the confines of history teaching, to basic questions of historical method and philosophy. History is 'the reconstruction of the past for its own sake, in the light of the evidence available to us'. It is not 'a source of lessons' or a 'prelude to current affairs.' In the pre-modern period, the study of the past may well have had some ulterior purpose. 'Examining the entrails of the past for the portents of the future is an age-old human activity, as is the nostalgia or personal security involved in looking at the past from the viewpoint of the present.' Now, however, history has been set on a sounder basis, 'as a discipline distinct from these activities'. It is true that 'general beliefs' or 'current debates' may initiate a line of enquiry, but such pressures are strictly external to the discipline. Once the topic is chosen, only the disciplines of the profession guide the historian, whose general ideas and interests play no part in the work of historical explanation. Since there is no intrinsic connexion between history and social interest, it follows that, in decisions about the curriculum of schools, the historian 'has no more authority ... to decide the weight to be given to different but equally respectable aspects' than (say) parents or politicians.

In several important respects, Beattie repeats the intellectual manoeuvres of others on the new right. Most important is the securing of his own position by reference to its compatibility with what are claimed to be purely professional standards, while at the same time the views of his opponents are exposed to attack on the grounds that they are ideologically-motivated interferences with the educational process. This is a difficult operation, especially as to carry it out he has to offend most of the tenets of

71

his own discipline, and in particular to restate a dichotomy between fact and interpretation which others – E.H. Carr, for instance – have long since thrown into question. He makes the claim that historical investigation is value-free, concerned with the reconstruction of the past in the light of impartially-considered evidence. The point has been answered by other historians, who do not reject the attempt to develop the fullest possible knowledge of any event in the past – merely deny that values of the present do not play a part in shaping the historian's research and final work. Indeed for one economic historian, 'history free of all values ... is a concept almost impossible to understand, for men will scarcely take the trouble to enquire laboriously into something which they set no value on'. Not only the choice of subject, but its treatment – the selection of evidence and the method of inquiry – are affected by the values and concerns of historians who live, social beings, in the midst of the conflicts of their times. Likewise, the empathy of historians, quickened by their participation in those conflicts, is central to their ability to create sustainable hypotheses about the life of the past. To speak of an historical imagination, born in such conflicts, is to understand much about the British historiography – E.P. Thompson, Barbara Taylor, John Foster, Gwyn A. Williams – of the last thirty years. Beattie would deny that in reputable history the present influences the past in these ways, just as he diminishes – with his mocking references to 'examining the entrails' – an entire classical and renaissance tradition that saw the consideration of the past as a means of making sense of the present day.

In the same way that Marenbon seeks to withdraw his discipline from contentious debate over value and purpose, into the impersonal authority of tradition, so Beattie severs the work of historians from any intrinsic connection with human need and interests, denying that they have a wider role in connecting the concerns of the present with those of other times. But if this is the case, on what grounds can the content of the history curriculum be determined – since choices must, on some basis, be arrived at? Historians, it is allowed, should have some say in these decisions – but no 'authoritative' one. The choice of content, in fact, must depend on the market – on parents who, Beattie assumes, will share his view of history. At this point, it is clear that Beattie is offering historians and history teachers a new role. Having been encouraged to suppress the values at work in their own research and writing, and to transform themselves into the practitioners of a value-free discipline, they are now to use their professional skills for a new purpose. Approvingly, in a footnote, Beattie summarizes David Cannadine's 1986 *Past and Present* Lecture, noting that, 'He deplores the extent to which British historians have ceased to glorify the greatness of Britain and have taken instead to "grubbing around in the archives".' That, Beattie hints, is why history is becoming an esoteric subject. In fact, the suggestion that history in schools should centre upon national themes is made at several points in the pamphlet. It refers disparagingly to the takeover of history by topics outside the British story, and itself celebrates history as 'the opportunity to appreciate a central inheritance,' making wistful reference to 'those British-based aspects which were once the main vehicles for an introduction to History'. Thus an argument which began with stern declarations about objectivity, and then proceeded to divest historians of their relationship to questions of value and meaning, concludes – via the introduction of the market forces which are going to determine the choice of subject and the balance of the curriculum – by pressing upon the historian that most value-laden role of all: a chronicler of one particular version of the British story.

From the work of Beattie and Marenbon – and of other writers in the CPS mould – it is possible to get a good idea of the model curriculum of the cultural right, and especially of the principles which underlie it. They are not attractive ones, and function more to defend traditional, exclusive kinds of education, rather than to make it useful to people's efforts to understand and to change their lives. Some central concerns emerge. First among them is the principle that their subjects have no basic connection with particular social struggles and interests. Second, and relatedly, there is distaste bordering on horror that concerns stemming from the lives of those now connected with education should play any part in reselecting and rejudging the elements of the curriculum. Finally, in place of these living interests, they seek to substitute a tradition, bulky with inherited authority, that will re-establish itself as the universal culture of the school, pushing to or over the margin all alternatives that rest on 'modish' interests like anti-sexism or anti-racism. Under cover of this tradition, they reintroduce or strengthen political and ideological tendencies that centre on issues of nation and authority. The intention of this section has been to demonstrate that these positions are not a convincing intellectual alternative to those that they criticize. However, the achievements of the right – even though it has been so confident in its assumption of the intellectual high ground – have not generally depended on cogency of argument, but rather upon skill in ideological contestation, and upon political initiative. The next, brief, concluding, section reviews some of its achievements in these respects. It also suggests what the right feels are the limits of its success, where tendencies to which it is hostile assume, despite its efforts, new influence within the education system.

Achievements and fears of the right

Some of the most powerful effects of the new right are, in any precise terms, incalculable. Around the specific impact of the legal changes it has inspired, lies a climate that has been deeply altered by its work. Consideration of the limits of the possible, moral judgements about right and wrong, assessments of the truth or falsity of claims about what has been achieved in schools have all been affected by the way the right has spread its ideas – downwards, through the press and particular parental campaigns; upwards, through lobbying and the careful circulation of material, to Parliament.

It is possible, though, within the general change, to specify some particular achievements. When Keith Joseph talks of history as the 'developing story of the nation', or Kenneth Baker of the English language as the force which has 'bound the people of England together', it is not certain whether the influence of pressure groups is directly at work, or whether ministers have spontaneously cast their views in this form. What is certain, at least, is that Joseph and Baker are able to speak with confidence in these ways, because of the work done by the right in establishing the centrality of certain cultural themes. Other achievements are more easily attributable. Many of the measures contained in the 1986 Education Act – those relating to sex education, police influence and political neutrality – were the specific results of right-wing lobbying. The proposals of the ERA for local management of schools, open enrolment, and opting out directly reflect the influence of the Hillgate Group and the Adam Smith Institute. The Act's establishment of a framework for a national curriculum and regular testing owes much to the relentless polemics of the right against the 'progressive' curriculum and the autonomy of teachers. Likewise, the proposals of the Adam Smith Institute, for changes in the system of certificating teachers, so as to undermine the claim that teaching is a specialized profession were later enunciated by Kenneth Baker. 'We want trainee teachers', he announced in February 1989 'to concentrate less on the history and sociology of education and more on how to cope with a classroom of fourteen-year olds'. The lines of communication between the pressure groups of the right and the drafters of legislation seem, on some issues, to be shorter than they have ever been.

Outside parliamentary politics, the right has been able to establish an educational agenda for large sections of the media – either directly, through articles by Scruton or Honeyford, for instance, or by identifying the issues which can serve as the focus for the education coverage of the Tory tabloids. Linked to the work with the media has been an ability to achieve a certain mobilization of parents. Despite media attention, when parent power has been an active force, it has not usually favoured the right: most parts of the country have seen parent campaigns against education cuts. What the right has been able to do, has been to target its strategy on particular weak points in the project of reform, where mistaken strategies or the great weight of opposing ideologies have led an equal opportunities policy into difficulty. Race and gender have been two of these links, and it is around these issues that the right's activists have swarmed and the general themes of its programme been able to cluster. Thus Baroness (Caroline) Cox was quick to support the 'parents' rights' campaign in Haringey against positive images of lesbians and gay men in the curriculum, and the Manchester and Dewsbury parents were assisted. Through these activities, which usually involve only a small number of parents, but whose

75

impact is enormously magnified by press attention, it has been possible for the right to create a powerful set of associations that link equal opportunity reform to 'minority' causes, and oppressive and inefficient procedures.

Spilling over from the campaigns of the right and the legislation they have led to, has been a deterrent effect that inhibits reforming tendencies in education. John Fairhall in *The Guardian* has claimed that clauses in the 1986 Act that forbade 'partisan' teaching are redundant, since they have not been used to intervene against teachers. Thus the argument can be made that the right's initiatives are not really relevant to what goes on in schools. Another way of understanding what Fairhall reports is that the reason the clauses have not been activated is that they have not needed to be. The press and the right have made the figure of the complaining parent a power in the land. Local authorities have maintained a watch on 'controversial' issues, and circulated schools with the texts of legislation on the matter. Teachers, in a similar process of self-censorship, tend to be more cautious than they once were in relating what they teach to issues seen as 'political'. Alongside this change has occurred another, equally significant. Under the incessant barrage that has been concentrated on state education, figures who, a decade previously, might have been solid supporters of the prevailing consensus of reform, have revised their estimate of it. It is not merely that they have become critical of schools, but that they have become critical within the system of ideas developed by the right. Thus journalists like *The Guardian*'s Melanie Phillips have echoed the right's claims that inner-city schools do not teach their pupils Standard English; Labour Council leaders have come to doubt the wisdom of ending habits of 'rote learning'. Much has been achieved by the right since the derided early days of the Black Papers.

The crowning achievement of the new right is the Education Reform Act. Yet it is exactly at this point, the passing of the Act, that the fears of the right – free market and cultural – are taking a new form. It was they who once criticized liberals as the sorcerers' apprentices whose callow experiments summoned up the demons of the left. Now, they fear that they themselves are becoming characters in a similar folktale, who, seeking deliverance from their oppressors, call for support upon a power whose intervention only imposes new forms of restraint. Since the framing of the legislation, the concerns of the right have become clear. Pamphlets from the Hillgate Group, and from the Centre for Policy Studies have both made the same point: through its emphasis on the national curriculum, the ERA will reinforce centralization. Far from enabling a great upsurge of consumer power, the Act, they fear, increases the influence of the state – and, more importantly, of the educational establishment within it. The state will not have a minimal role; it will not limit itself to clearing aside what obstructs the operation of market principles, nor to securing a minimum level of educational 'grounding', beyond which diversity can flourish. It will be a lot more directive than that, and its policies, think the right, will only 'entrench the orthodoxies' of education, and raise again the dangers of producer control. 'If', writes Sheila Lawlor, 'the content of the proposed new curriculum merely reflects the views of members of the 'education service' – teachers, their unions, LEA's, educational theorists and, worst of all, HMI – then the national curriculum, instead of serving to raise standards, will lower them.' For the new right, thus, the passing of the Act is not the summit of its achievement, but one more stage along the way. The struggle is not over, and powerful enemies remain.

The disputes over issues like this are not at all superficial; they reveal deep-rooted differences within Conservatism, between what can briefly and with some imprecision, be called traditional and modernizing tendencies. These differences have until now been obscured by the polemical drive of Tory policy: new right ideas (of both a cultural and a free market sort) have combined with those of modernization to subject the work of teachers, the nature of the curriculum and the organization of schools to sustained attack. The right has been quite willing to tolerate an increase in the powers of the state in order to crush its opponents. Now that it is a matter of developing a positive and comprehensive set of policies, tensions arise, and in doing so reveal the incoherences of the Conservative programme. Thus, many Conservatives – Kenneth Baker among them – are willing to make use of the right's slogans to strengthen their position within the party, and to gain tactical advantage over their opponents outside. But they do not see in the programme of the right anything that can inspire the curricular change that they think necessary if education is to become a means of inspiring and sustaining economic growth. For this latter task, they are quite willing to look outside the intellectual traditions of the right, and to seek a careful relationship with tendencies in education which the right has spent many years denouncing. The next chapter examines what is involved in the resulting process of Conservative-led modernization.

3

Conservative modernization

The previous chapter described two aspects of the educational
right. One – the cultural right – had a patriarchal sternness. The
second displayed the eagerness of free market thought.
Reverting to the image with which this book began, they could
be said to be the Janus-faces of Conservatism. Except that the
image does not quite fit. Conservatism in education – as
elsewhere – is three-headed, rather than double-faced. The
point can be made in this way: the tendency of free market
thought, supported in practice by cultural rightists like Scruton,
is to insist that the future of the British economy is dependent
almost entirely upon free enterprise and privatization –
economic planning of any sort would play little part. It is from
this perspective that the Adam Smith Institute approaches
education. But in this attitude free market thinkers and
traditionalists stand at some distance from a third important
aspect of Conservatism, that could roughly be described as a
modernizing tendency – not because it is the only current which
wishes to achieve economic regeneration and modernizing
change in education, but because more deliberately than any
other it seeks to intervene in many areas of social life with the
prime and specific intention of achieving them. This does not
mean that it wishes to return to an economic and political
strategy of corporatism: it is intent, rather, on creating an
'enterprise economy' and on reducing union influence, and thus
borrows much from the free market programme. It does,
however, intend that the pace and the content of change should
be shaped by state intervention. In education this entails the
belief that the content of the curriculum is far too important to
be left to the autonomy of the individual school. The free
marketeers and the cultural right may see the state's role as
essentially negative, in putting down all those forces –
bureaucratic or insurgent – which in Scruton's words 'threaten

the freedom and trouble the life of the ordinary citizen'. The modernising tendency, however, has a more positive conception of the state's powers. Strong government action is needed – particularly in an area like education – to correct historic weaknesses and set down the clear outlines of a path along which the system should go.

The intellectual features of this tendency are shaped by a sense of economic crisis – a sense that grows from the acute difficulties of the present, into a response to an entire century of retarded development. This deeper level of response not only searches through the indices of productivity and investment for explanations of decline, but also probes the faults in the national culture that have led to the near-fatal failings of the late twentieth century.

Britain, it is noted, has experienced since 1870 'one of the largest relative declines in economic strength ever recorded'. Since 1945 the pace of decline has increased. One particular explanation for the present stage of crisis has become almost canonical on the political right and centre: 'the thesis that the pressure of popular demand for a universal system of social security (including full employment) created insurmountable long-term deficiencies in the economy which lie at the heart of our present troubles'. Around this fundamental claim circle others, that gloss it in particular ways: a bloated public sector has drained investment funds from industry; productivity, hampered by union power, has grown too slowly; full employment policies have tilted the balance of forces in the economy too far towards the interests of labour. From these starting points, Conservative modernization devises policies intended to break out of decline, and to transform the British economy, under a right-wing star. Modernization, from this point of view, entails not simply a programme of investment, but an eradication of ingrained habits – those of labour and those of leading sections of society.

Over the last decade, there has been a search for a 'cause of causes', for a special factor in British life which has allowed so many wrongs to go uncorrected for so long. Some, influentially, like Martin Wiener, have found it in the nature of English culture, and, in particular, of its education system. 'Bourgeois values', Wiener quotes Keith Joseph, 'have never shaped thought and institutions as they have done in some countries.' Instead, the culture of the world's first industrial society was, and is, affected by the potent residue of an older social order. Aristocratic, or more properly, landed capitalist influences marked the culture of industrial Britain in its formative years, and vitiated the raw energies of entrepreneurialism. The sons of those who grew rich from the Industrial Revolution received in their public schools and universities a disabling humanist education that, in Barnett's words, 'posed an entirely false antithesis between the subjects fit for enriching the mind, cultivating the reason and inspiring the moral sense, and those other subjects held to amount to no more than the mundane nuts and bolts of a narrow professional training'. From such a basis, the 'primitive' technologies and methods of organization that characterized the Industrial Revolution in Britain could never be sufficiently transcended to allow effective competition with Germany, the United States and the long trail of industrializing powers which followed them. It is of this experience that Lord Young, the leading 'modernizer' of Mrs Thatcher's Cabinet, spoke, in claiming: 'Sometimes the government is accused of wanting to return to Victorian values. In education this is anything but the truth. In fact many of the problems we face today go back directly to the values of the Victorians.' Behind Young, though not necessarily sharing all his enthusiasm for an enterprise economy, stood an extensive lobby for change in education: academic currents that had diagnosed the causes of the British malaise, some industrialists – in large companies such as British Gas, British Telecom and ICI – and above all the Manpower Services Commission, described by Keith Joseph as a proxy for employers. Pressure from this lobby initiated educational programmes that have grown beyond their vocational origins to have a general effect on educational practice. None of this work takes 'academic' education, as the cultural right would understand it, as its model.

At this point, we confront the central difference between two major strands of Conservative education policy. So far as the curriculum is concerned, the emphasis of the cultural right – supported by free market groups like the ASI – is upon continuity. That of people like Young is upon breaking all those ancient shackles which now chain down the potential for economic and for individual development. Thus, while no opponent of selection, the modernizing tendency has no time for the grammar school tradition. Unlike the cultural right, it considers it to be part of the problem, not the solution. It is thoroughly critical of the anti-industrial values of a liberal education: the state schools of the present century have reproduced many of the failings of the public schools that some of them have tried to emulate, and have preserved a rigid distinction between high-status academic knowledge and low-status practical training. Adhering to a book-bound curriculum, they offer to students an education which many find irrelevant and demotivating. The modernizers, by contrast, present their programme as a means not only of serving industry but – by knocking down the academic/practical barrier – of democratizing knowledge, and of enabling students to demonstrate kinds of achievement which the old education neither fostered nor recognized.

This, though, is only half the burden of the modernizers' arguments. For them, state education combines the worst of the old with the worst of the reforming new. The shackles they want to throw off are not only those forged by a nineteenth-century intelligentsia. It is because of the character and direction of *modern* state education that the school has become what one compilation of industrialists' views calls 'an adventure playground for educationalists', in which a 'laudable compassion for disadvantaged pupils may have produced a "softness" which is markedly at variance with the competitive requirements of industry'. Thanks to a school culture that combines lukewarm attitudes to science with an anti-industrial bias, 'many young people [are] more interested in courses which they feel would help them reform and heal society' than in becoming technologists and engineers. Alongside the 'democratic' claims of the modernizers runs a determination to put an end to these more malign effects of progressive reform, and to establish at the heart of education new kinds of attitude and purpose.

It is a project that needs to be seen against a wider background, a vaster educational process that runs through the capillaries of British society: a general Conservative effort, expressed in many different areas of policy, to re-educate the population, whether as workers or as citizens. This process has many strands, most of which converge on a single, broad and unifying theme: the fostering of a mentality that looks to individual initiative as the prime means of advance, and that forsakes belief in collective action either by trade unionists or a politically active citizenry. The hammer blows directed against trade unions, the centralization of political life and the authoritarianism of much social policy are one side of this process. The other is the enlargement of consumer freedoms and market influence which goes with every new measure of privatization and deregulation. Translated into terms of 'initiative' and 'enterprise' – and interwoven with the concerns introduced by the cultural right – this form of re-education runs through the entire programme for modernizing the school.

Yet remarkably this project has proved attractive to many of those associated with education reform, who have accepted elements of its diagnosis and welcomed much of what it says about curriculum change, even while they have dissented from and tried to modify other parts of its programme. They give modernization this reception because it draws its criticisms and prescriptions from a repertoire which, historically, has been more the property of reforming tendencies than of thinkers of the Black Paper variety. Its demand, for instance, that schools should encourage other kinds of achievement than the academic is one that has been made widely by reformers. Its preference for experience-based learning likewise echoes reforming traditions, and its comments on the irrelevance of education to the lives of many students also strikes a familiar note. Of course, there is much suspicion about the general purposes of the modernizers' programme of change, but, on the whole, it is one that can be worked with. Its concerns, unlike those of the right, do not to seek a confrontation with reform at the everyday level of classroom working. Indeed, in some respects, the modernizers appear to base their changes on the best of current, progressive-influenced practice.

The following sections try first of all to understand this *rapprochement*: to explain why modernization makes use of some progressive themes and what it does to alter them. Having tried to explain, they will go on to criticize. Progressive moderniz- ation, or modernized progressivism, is based on the collapse of a tradition that was not without its radical elements into a project which serves Conservative social ends. It is part of the process by which educators are rendering themselves incapable of recognizing a bad educational principle when they see one. Faced with the threat of the new right, they welcome the alternative embrace of modernisation. A critique of this process seems to me essential: educationists are adept at finding 'spaces' to work in. They eye each centralizing government initiative at first with horror, fury and awe, as a juggernaut which will surely crush those few remaining shoots of autonomous, grassroots creativity in the system. After a time, the awe lessens; denunciation diminishes from an angry shouting to an occasional murmur. There begins a period of calculation. How can this juggernaut, which obviously is not going to go away, be worked with? In what areas might it require the services of the existing order? How can its more unfortunate extremes be modified? And also, perhaps – base thought, arising from the depths of disillusionment with reform – to what extent might there be something in this juggernaut after all? Might not its programme, suitably tempered, answer the problems of curriculum and underachievement that have persisted for so long? Criticism is now replaced by a policy of judicious involvement: the scheme has been accepted as inevitable, and the issue is now to make it work in a way which is congruent with prevailing practice. Thus, damage can be limited, the best of the new absorbed, and continuity preserved.

Such is the way of the world as the more sanguine voices of reform describe it. Such also are the fears of the Centre for Policy Studies, which thinks that the 'educational establishment' is only accepting change so that, ultimately, things will remain the same, with the same kinds of people in control. There is some truth in both opinions. What they miss is the extent of the adaptation to government policy which is the price that a strategy of judicious involvement pays. Continually – in order to maintain some influence – giving ground on issues of principle, the institutions that have sustained reform have become incapable of setting out ideas that could sustain an alternative agenda. It is with this sad process in mind that this chapter shortly attempts a critical encounter with some of the ideas that animate Conservative modernisation. It is aiming to demonstrate what many who engage with this programme of change seem to have overlooked:

the narrowness of its conceptions of knowledge; the limitations of its claim to promote equal opportunity; and, most of all, the utter meagreness of the ideas of human potential than run through its claim to be developing a better, more fulfilling education.

Incorporating progressive education

Since the late 1970s it has become customary for major documents on education to begin with a review of the comparative position of the British economy. Thus *Better Schools*, the White Paper of 1985, begins with an account of the circumstances that necessitate change, and in particular relates the issue of standards to that of international competition. Whereas the reference point for the new right was the real or imagined level of standards *in the past*, the White Paper makes its criticisms 'not least in the light of what is being achieved in other countries'. It goes on to specify some of the 'qualities and skills required for work in the technological age', making clear that the 3Rs are far too limited a basis on which to rest such qualities, which centre on the 'enterprise and adaptability' that is necessary 'to increase young people's chances of finding employment or creating it for themselves and others'. Later, the document reports those 'capabilities' which employers 'look to the schools to have fostered in recruits to industry and commerce'. Employers' organizations:

> gave widespread support for a broadly-based education in which academic achievement should be complemented by the capacity to apply knowledge and by the development of personal qualities and skills, including motivation and commitment, self-discipline and reliability, confidence, enthusiasm and initiative, flexibility and the ability to work both individually and as part of a team. Employers urged that schools should set out to equip pupils with the knowledge, skills and attitudes needed for adult and working life; most also stressed the need for greater emphasis on the relevance and practical applications of what pupils learn. Competence in reading, writing and oral skills was seen as the essential minimum; and it was also regarded as important that both pupils and teachers should have greater awareness of the wealth-creating function of industry and commerce.

These comments are miles away from the programme of the new right. A number of points can be made about them. First, that reading, writing and numerical skills are merely seen as minimum achievements – albeit essential ones. Second – much perhaps to the disgust of a commentator like Marenbon – they are valued equally with oral and 'social' skills. Third, that there are persistent references to qualities of attitude – among them 'flexibility' and 'initiative' – that rank equally with those related to knowledge and skills. Fourth, there is the emphasis on the 'practical applications of what students learn'. Finally, comes the ideologically explicit demand for an education system thoroughly appreciative of the importance of enterprise. Other official or semi-official documents made the same kind of points. One of the most influential was *Competence and Competition*, a report prepared for the MSC in 1984, that compared education and training in Britain with that of West Germany, Japan and the United States. Like *Better Schools*, though more aggressively, it referred to failures in the teaching of the 3Rs, and then went on to indicate the need for an education of a new type, appropriate to a modernised system of production. 'Paradoxically', it claimed, the sharp decline in the need for the craft skills associated with the apprenticeship model of training, 'opens the door to a ... new emphasis on *competences*', that included qualities such as the ability to work in a team, flexibility and the desire to learn. This last point was especially important. 'Employees need to want to learn', so that retraining becomes almost a reflex reaction to changing technologies and employment patterns.

At this point, we arrive at the paradox of Conservative-led modernization, where, rather than flaunt reactionary colours, official commentaries and critiques recall in ironic and startling ways, the polemics of earlier responses to the condition of state education. For there was a tradition, well-rooted in Britain though derived in important respects from European and American thinking, that contrasted the archaism of the school with the requirements of modern society. It had defined itself as 'the new education', which sought to renovate the curriculum and pedagogy of the school. From this perspective, it deplored the split between academic and vocational education, and the high value assigned to 'bookishness' at the expense of an education that tried to make connections with 'real life'. It valued other qualities in the student besides academic attainment, and was committed to a programme of activity-based, collaborative learning. Yet despite these highly functional attributes, it had not, up until now, been the favoured educational cause of an industrial lobby. To set down its name is to explain why: 'progressive education' – precisely that tendency which for decades had provided so many monsters to populate the right's demonology.

As we have already seen, progressivism was held responsible by the right for many of the ills of education. Allegedly, it downplayed the importance of the factual basis of learning, created social relations in the classroom that prevented learning, and, by stressing the sacrosanct needs of the child, neglected the importance of transmitting the essential principles of the national culture. Above all, perhaps, it sacrificed quality for equality: by insisting on equal treatment for all children, it diverted attention from the needs of elite groups. Certainly, these complaints were right to identify something radical in progressivism. Despite its diverseness, it can still be termed a modernizing tendency of a broadly left-wing kind. In the 1920s – its classical period – it had been critical of 'industrial society' and social authoritarianism. As taken up in the 1960s by promoters of reform, it added to these commitments a concern to eradicate educational disadvantage. From the early part of the century right through to the 1970s, 'progressivism', taking its stand on the need of students fully to express their potential, had counterposed its views to the requirements of an economic system which was run on quite different principles. As one progressive headteacher put it in 1976:

'If our objective is to assist the students to take increasing control of their own destinies, to question assumptions, to solve problems by being inventive and trained to envisage speculative alternatives, we are bound to meet conflict with an industrial society that sees schools principally as the sorting house for employment.'

How, then, with this record of critique, could elements of progressivism be incorporated into a new vocationalist orthodoxy? The most convincing answer is that for a long period it was the only tendency to address curricular and pedagogic questions basic to the efficiency of a mass education system in a developed capitalist society. Any such system will need ideas for securing students' motivation to learn, and thus for devising curricula that are relevant to their lives. Any such society will need from its workforce and citizens a range of skills and qualities that cannot be developed within the bounds of an academic schooling. These are among the reasons for progressivism's attractiveness to educational policy-makers – an attractiveness that has lasted several decades, and is not likely to be dispelled by the critiques of a new right which does not even recognize the existence of the problems the progressives address.

Progressive education's assimilation into official policy has at different times taken different forms. In the particular conditions of the 1960s and 1970s, for instance, its influence lay not only in its attention to the details of teaching and learning, but also in its more general concerns for social justice and a particular type of student self-development. Over the last decade, the assimilation of what is thought useful in progressivism into the new mainstream has been a more discriminating affair. The keywords of progressive pedagogy have circulated as never before, and much of its practice has been embodied in the 'revolution in education and training' that has developed in the 1980s. Other aspects, though – especially those connected with progressivism's social philosophy – are less in vogue. Given these more critical features of its tradition, there could be no question of progressivism's wholesale take-up by industrially-orientated modernizers. Selective assimilation was a more appropriate strategy. In the middle 1970s, right at the centre of the educational apparatus, among the national inspectorate, such a process got underway. Until then, wrote one inspector, discussion about education was 'characterised by a kind of two-party oppositional politics'. On one side, was a progressive or 'liberal romantic' perspective, that 'celebrated self-expression, individual autonomy, first-hand experience, discovery learning and personal growth'. It emphasized the 'process of learning rather than its products' and aimed at 'a much more equal partnership between teachers and students'. In sharp contrast, existed an 'elementary' tradition, that viewed

88

the curriculum as 'a repository of essential subjects and skills which need to be handed down ... by teachers in an orderly, systematic way'. Neither of these incompatibles was acceptable, and so a third, synthetic perspective – 'liberal pragmatism' – emerged, with strong support from the Inspectorate, to 'set the agenda for discussion and policy-making in English ... education'. The writer suggested that liberal pragmatism 'holds a middle ground position, viewing the curriculum as a set of learning experiences largely ... determined by teachers, but respecting to some extent both the individuality of children and the importance of cultural transmission'. It 'uses children's knowledge and interest as starting points and contributions to ongoing work' but 'shapes and refines children's experience along teacher-centred lines'.

The criticisms that the middle way makes of progressivism are not without substance. It is true that the 'liberal romantic' tradition has been inattentive to the problems of an education that does not bring the culture of the student into relationship with formally-organized knowledge. But the significance of the liberal pragmatist critique is less pedagogical than social. Whatever its failings, progressivism had some democratic and egalitarian content: its educational principles were intended not just as better ways of organizing a classroom, but as embodiments of alternative ways of organizing social relationships, and of furthering the interest of particular social groups. It was this wider interest that was particularly vulnerable in the 'pragmatic' modification of progressivism.

The point can be seen with special clarity in the Inspectorate's approach to the teaching of English, set out in 1984. As Marenbon realized, English was of all subjects the one most closely related to liberal romanticism. Powerful traditions of English teaching had insisted that it should be organized around a defence of individual values and marginal social traditions against the crushing cultural weight of industrial society. The influence of these trends was pervasive – they were the air that English teachers breathed, in a process so customary and natural as to be beyond normal questioning. Within that atmosphere were developed curricula that encouraged some kind of critical understanding of cultural forms and social issues, and sought to cultivate values that often stood in opposition to those prevailing outside the gates of the school. It was from this tradition, so integral a part of English teaching, that the Inspectorate turned tacitly away. They endorsed an English devoid of any sharp social concern, nowhere blander and more banal than in its description of the lives and needs of 16-year-old students:

> At 16, pupils have reached the end of the statutory period of schooling. Some will continue their school education to a higher level; some will enter further education or training; some will enter the world of work, and some, sadly, will fail to do so. All, whatever their educational or vocational future, will face the personal and social demands of adult life. For all these purposes, they need competence in a range of uses of English.

The neutral tones of these statements of the apparently obvious mask a certain complacency with the present way of the world, which no adverbs of compassion can do very much to mitigate. More to the point is their definition of English in terms of 'competence' – a word that evokes so much of the flavour of educational modernization. 'Achieving competence in the many and varied uses of our language' is how the document's first sentence defines the aims of English teaching, and the word is used repeatedly thereafter. The overall effect is to promote an instrumental concern with language-in-use above interest in language as a cultural process, in which are expressed different experiences and values. Yet, in this version of the subject, many of the forms of progressive discourse are retained. The student is seen as an active user of language; language is defined as a wide-ranging set of competences, and there is careful recognition of non-standard forms. But the historical essence of the subject – its critical concern with culture and value – has been spirited away, in a paradigm of the kinds of reinterpretation that 'liberal pragmatism' has made of the progressive tradition. English is diminished to a concern with skills and capability, alongside references only of the most conventional sort to 'imaginative literature' and to study of the media.

The efforts to reorientate subject areas particularly affected by progressivism did not remain at the level of argument. The 'new' education 'was characterised too, by a concern for planning and policy-making at school and local authority levels'. Whereas progressivism stressed that the uniqueness of each child's experience required that the teacher be given professional autonomy in devising programmes to meet individual need, its successor took a different view. Change required not greater local initiative in planning educational projects, but increased central control of curricula and teaching methods. The creativity of teachers was to be exercised at the level of carrying out the plans of others. The Inspectorate document, prefiguring the national curriculum, specified targets for students to achieve at set ages. In this it formed one link in a newly reinforced system of educational surveillance. By the mid-1980s, the work of teachers became subject to a degree of guidance of a sort unknown since the early part of the century. Detailed criteria for the 'delivery' of the curriculum were an integral part of reforms such as the General Certificate of Secondary Education, the Technical and Vocational Education Initiative, and the post-16 Certificate of Pre-Vocational Education. Inspectorate guidelines covered a greater and greater area of the work of the school. The 'programmes of study' integral to the national curriculum promised to make such guidance more authoritative and more detailed. Powers of educational initiative passed over almost entirely to LEAs and to school managements, who in turn tended to be prompted by government thinking. The curriculum influence of teachers' organizations dwindled with the abolition of the Schools Council in 1984. That of classroom teachers declined less visibly but just as drastically: neither the ideological climate, nor the continual battles over cuts and pay increases created a mood that favoured teacher-led experiment. After the ending of the pay dispute, Baker's new conditions of service decisively imposed managerial authority on the school. The requirement placed upon teachers to attend management-initiated meetings after four o'clock and outside the teaching year set up an effective transmission belt for a curriculum development whose impetus came largely from the centre. The frequency and sheer pace of the new initiatives was enough, in a depressed staffroom climate, to render opposition insubstantial. Never can so many changes have been demanded of a teaching force, so subdued in its own educational thinking.

In these ways was developing a new education, that utilized a version of progressivism. Closely monitored and stripped of its radical parts – its tendency to promote democracy in schools or to encourage social criticism – it was available for use within a particular kind of modernized curriculum. Many attractive aspects of educational change, such as the increase in parental involvement in primary education and the search for new ways of recording student achievement, owed much to earlier progressive challenges to the usual pattern of home-school relations and the exam-centred curriculum. Albeit alongside a heavier workload for teachers, they offered a closer attention to the learning process than that of the chalk-and-talk pedagogy which was still the learning medium in many classrooms. Something similar can be said of the proposals for national curricula in maths, science and primary English, published in the latter part of 1988: they do not step back from 'liberal pragmatism'. They, too endorse an experience-based learning; they are concerned with the learning process and conceptual development in a way that Sheila Lawlor would find most disturbing. Their publication, like other developments of the later 1980s, poses a question that flickers just beneath the surface of much discussion among educational innovators: that of whether a Conservative government, in many ways so ready to tolerate or incite the most traditional of educational views, is nevertheless willing to preside over an extensive process of curriculum change, that can with justice – though some puzzlement – be labelled progressive.

There are those, certainly, who see the modernizing tendency within government policy as something that is entirely congruent with the progressive tradition, and who give it support against the Conservative right. Ian Jamieson, long-time promoter of links between school and work and now 'BP lecturer in Education and Industry' at the University of Bath is one who has made this choice, and who detects a similar movement on the part of other educators. In an article co-authored with Tony Watts, he writes:

'One of the fascinating features ... of the enterprise and schools-industry movements in general has been the extent to which they have won the support of many teachers who were

92

initially suspicious or hostile. This is largely because, despite their political origins, they have been developed in ways which have caught the essence of what many progressive educationalists would regard as a good education.'

The right's insistence on a subject-based curriculum imperils this 'hard-won progress'.

Jamieson and Watts have made explicit what has become a general tendency in education, from union leaders and labour politicians to classroom teachers. Initially through a policy of support for a lesser evil, but more recently through a growing conviction about the intrinsic value of modernizing change, they have become engaged with reforms whose origins, as Watts and Jamieson indicate, lie either in Labour's 'Great Debate' or more recent Conservative policy. They seek to use the opportunities that have sprung up around the modernizing project to consolidate progressive trends and block the right's advance. Thus virtually all have supported the proposals of the Black Report on testing – both because they are preferable to the pen and paper tests favoured by the new right, and because they propose elegant solutions to the problem of integrating systematic assessment into the normal work of the classroom. The function of testing in relation to curricular and cultural uniformity and inter-school competition tends to be played down. Likewise, thousands of teachers devote their efforts to making a success of vocational projects that, though they are doubtless an activity-based, relevant alternative to the subject-centred, desk-bound curricula of the past, still operate within the range of official ideas about enterprise and the economy.

Many of those involved would see their work as a kind of civilizing subversion, that tames the wilder excesses of Conservative policy by exposing them to the influence of the progressive tradition. But there is a price to be paid for this activity: 'subversion', such as it is, takes place on the ground established by Conservative reform. Although the application of reform is open to amendment, its guiding, organizing principles remain, and are absorbed in the practice of those who implement them.

This tendency is reinforced by a failure critically to engage with the process by which keywords of progressive education have been subsumed in a different discourse, in which their meanings have been transformed. Those who wish to undermine the Conservative project from within find that the reference points of their own position are no longer stable. 'Creativity', 'individuality' and 'knowledge' are terms which, since the heyday of the 1960s, have changed their meaning. Exposed for years to the discourse of entrepreneurialism, processed through curricular projects that conceive of knowledge as a set of market-oriented skills, and self-development as the process through which these skills are acquired, these words have themselves, to borrow a phrase from espionage, been turned. The critiques that follow address the new meanings that have been created, and aim to show the shortcomings of the ideas that lie behind them – ideas which reveal so much both about the grander claims of the modernizing programme, and about the paucity of the intellectual case its defenders are making.

Culture, democracy and the individual

Two decades ago, the Plowden Report on primary education marked the high tide of official support for progressive education. Against the regimentation of the elementary school, which centred on the transmission of a body of knowledge to a group of pupils seen as a uniform mass, Plowden, was concerned to identify the specific characteristics and needs of each individual child. 'The school' it said, 'sets out deliberately to devise the right environment for children, to allow them to be themselves and to develop in the way and at the pace appropriate to them.' Of course, this idea of 'being themselves' – as Valerie Walkerdine has shown – possessed a strong normalizing element, so that only certain kinds of self-expression were in practice acceptable; but even when restricted in this way, the progressive idea of the individual was expressed in humanist, rather than directly utilitarian terms. Plowden argued that 'the best preparation for being a happy and useful man and woman is to live fully as a child'. 'Primary children', it asserted, 'need to be themselves, to live with other children and with grown-ups, to learn from their environment, to enjoy the present, to get ready for the future, to create and to love, to learn to face adversity, to behave responsibly, in a word, to be human beings.'

The primary school, in the 1960s, was the main focus and generator of influential models of education. In the era of Baker and Joseph – of training for responsible citizenship and the world of work – the emphasis has shifted to the secondary years. Here selfhood has now a very different language. 'For us', Kenneth Baker told his party conference in 1986, 'education must fulfil the individual's potential, not stifle it in the name of egalitarianism'. White Papers demand a 'climate in which people can be motivated and their creative capacity harnessed'. Businessmen complain that education 'diminishes the life chances and inhibits the talents of many people'. The new education, with equal opportunity at its heart, will ensure that 'the achievements of all, whatever their race, sex or class, can be raised'. The language is excited, promise-crammed, attentive to individual need.

But what, on second hearing, is the meaning of the terms – 'individual', 'creative' and so on – with which the discourse is saturated? How much do they overlap with, or abandon, the meanings of Plowden? 'Creative' by now is fairly familiar: it relates to entrepreneurial endeavour, rather than to the imaginative qualities which it *used* to denote. 'Individual' is used in a more complex way. In part, it validates inequality – the needs of the individual requiring increased distinction between the kinds of education available to students of different abilities. But it also suggests the kinds of learner whom education is addressing – both the personal qualities he or she already possesses, and those the school should be producing in them. In this sense it is very revealing of the ideas of culture and of human development that underlie the modernizing aspects of the Conservative programme.

Its conception of the individual is, in cultural terms, a very abstract one. Conservatives of the Scruton kind write about *belonging*; for them, individuals are constituted by the culture they live in, and the tasks of politics relate to maintaining the cohesion of that culture. It is from this angle that they view history, literature, leisure and all the transactions of everyday life. All are given a significance, that links in one direction with the nature of individuality, and in the other with the political order. Baker himself is happy on occasion to toy with views like these. No minister is more fulsome in evoking images of an idyllic Englishness, product of 'a unique and beautiful country', or in praising the English language, 'our mother tongue ... our greatest asset as a nation ... the essential ingredient of the Englishness of England'; nor more immersed in an imperial imagination, whether he is evoking the 'fever trees of the Limpopo', or the 'teeming presence of India'.

Baker is concerned, albeit gesturally, with the cultural medium through which individuality is lived. The themes of the modernizing tendency, on the other hand, are in an important sense acultural. 'Belonging', 'community' and the problems of social solidarity are not at its centre, and its conception of the individual is correspondingly non-concrete. It quietly assumes the unproblematic existence of a unified national culture, but lacks the urgent assertiveness of the right that such a culture must be transmitted to all social groups. Thus, questions of culture operate more as an implicit background to modernization than as immediate, strongly-argued themes. Nevertheless, behind most official accounts of – say – the national curriculum, there are understandings at work which both unself-consciously present the culture embodied in that curriculum as universal, and unceremoniously neglect the cultures and understandings which students bring to the school. As one of Baker's consultative documents on the ERA puts it, the national curriculum will ensure

> 'that all pupils, regardless of sex, ethnic origin and geographical location, have access to broadly the same good and relevant curriculum and programmes of study, which include the key content, skills and processes which they need to learn and which ensure that the content and teaching of the various elements of the national curriculum bring out their relevance to and links with pupils' own experiences and their practical applications and continuing value to adult and working life.'

The sentence is interesting for the Procrustean argument that underlies it: it standardizes the life of the student so as to fit him or her to a one-size national curriculum. Interesting in this respect is the use of 'regardless' in connection with 'relevant'. The curriculum, apparently, will be relevant to everyone, even though it will have no regard to where they live, what sex they are, and what their racial background is: it will be the same for all, and yet relevant to all! There is a striking confidence that the learning programme devised by the curriculum planners will be fully congruent with the experience of students, alongside an equally striking lack of interest in what that experience might be. That students differ in what their society has made of them; that the sexual, class or racial prisms through which they view the world affect their attitudes to learning and their conceptions of relevance are not important matters. Because their lives are seen as empty and cultureless, the national curriculum seems all the more unproblematic. It can appear as the embodiment of a universal culture, rather than the very particular selection of elements, made from the dominant cultural viewpoint, that it does comprise. Thus the 1988 Kingman Report on *The Teaching of the English Language* can describe Standard English, in quite uncomplicated fashion, as the 'language which we all have in common ... a great social bank on which we all draw'. Its dominant status is nothing to do with its links with a particular class: 'it is the fact of being the written form which establishes it as the standard'. In these ways an argument resting upon suppositions about a national unity of experience, inhibits consideration of difference and inequality. Even the best of the official documents produced in the wake of the ERA – that of the working party on English in primary schools that was chaired by Black Paper editor Brian Cox, and that reflected the influence of social linguistics – does not escape this tendency. Remarkably, in view of Cox's background, it is sensitive to the relationship between students' language and their sense of social identity, and aware in a way that Kingman, and Marenbon, are not to the fact that Standard English is a social dialect, as well as a language of learning. Still, in all its references to the uses of that social dialect, the emphasis falls on its powers of communication, rather than its role in the communication of power.

Despite the problems that it has with the concept of individuality, in other ways the new education seeks to shape and monitor personal development more attentively than ever before. Though the cultural aspects of the individual are scarcely glimpsed, the qualities required by the world of work are put in much more concrete terms. The report on *Competence and Competition* puts the issue most clearly, in identifying a difference between the aims of education as previously accepted in Britain, and those promoted in other countries, which 'consciously' include 'such training objectives as teamwork, flexibility and the desire to learn'. In Britain, the tendency has been to regard them as 'personal qualities' rather than vocational outcomes. Qualities which have previously been considered 'personal' – in the sense that Plowden's conceptions were 'personal' – should be relocated in a different context, with a highly pronounced vocational stress. On the 'desire to learn', for instance, the report notes that:

> the difficulty is not that people do not want to learn. Britain has one of the most highly developed adult education systems in the world. The success of the Open University is just one of the many indications that the desire to learn continues. The WEA still has 170,000 members.... What seems to have happened is that people want to learn but they perceive that learning to be related to their private interests or to matters which make them more independent of their employers.

This has to change. Desire for knowledge and satisfaction with learning must be transferred to the area of 'competent performance' in employment. Human development is to be relocated in occupational training.

Nor is this a change only at the level of statements of intent. A pedagogy has arisen that pays the most detailed attention to means by which a new sense of self can be inculcated in working-class students, by means of what Phillip Cohen has called a 'micro-technology of self-improvement'. The 'Social and Life Skills' courses that are now widespread in schools and colleges teach 'techniques of impression management designed to help students project a positive self-image to employers'. In doing so, they disparage the cultures of home and street as obstacles to successful employment and encourage 'the crassest and most individualist strategies of adaptation to mass unemployment.' In this sense, it is possible to speak of the 'new person' that modernized education means to create: eager to adapt, convinced of the rewards of individual enterprise, accepting and enacting the values of the business climate around them.

There is a problem, however, with a stress like this. Conservative ideologists themselves are aware that an educational – as well as a wider cultural – hegemony requires a broader base than vocationalism can provide. Conservative Britain proliferates with schemes for the creation of work-orientated personalities, and its leaders are skilful with a rhetoric of standards and excellence. They are not so comfortable with those aspects of culture which establish a regime's claim to a higher legitimacy, as a guardian angel of creativity. In a speech on the teaching of English in late 1986, Baker, with an eye on credentials of this kind, insisted that 'the new and proper emphasis on the application and practical aspects of subjects ... should not lead to any diminution in the magic and potency of literature'. In his earlier incarnation as chair of the MSC, Lord Young pleaded with an audience, 'I hope you will not consider me a philistine .... I recognise the need for artistic endeavour, for the enhancement of our cultural life, for a need to give us all the interest and the interests to spend our ever-increasing leisure.' Both men, aware that reference to 'employers' needs' would not on this occasion clinch the argument, looked elsewhere, outside the world of work, to discover qualities that contribute to the education of the whole person. But rather than presenting with modernist enthusiasm the qualities that a new education could develop in students, they fell back on the rhetorical conventions of a not-very-recent past, which are quite unable to address the cultural experience of the late twentieth century. Baker's invocation of the 'magic of literature' is a weary trope, that places literature outside social life. It belongs, like many of his cultural reference points, to an antiquated literary tradition. The paradox is striking. His government has fostered one of the great modern attempts to transform ideas and sensibilities. In all its efforts the role of the media has been crucial, in building up the great demons and desires of popular culture in the Thatcher era. By the mid-1990s, television and radio will have been subjected to increasingly direct commercial influence. The dominance of purely financial criteria for programme-making will lead to the same downmarket spiralling as that which has taken the tabloid press to new depths. Yet Baker, a leading member of a Cabinet which has set all this in motion, speaks warily of the 'marshy ground' of 'modern culture' and appeals to the magic of literature against a TV culture 'much of which is mundane and brain-numbing'. This disparity, between a traditionalist idea of culture, set out in its Sunday best on ministerial speech days, and the cultural activities more usually associated with Thatcherism, indicates something incomplete and – even in its own terms – unsatisfactory about the Conservative programme. In the Jekyll and Hyde *mélange* which is the rhetoric of Kenneth Baker, the Jekyll-Baker of cultural tradition steps back in horror from the Baker-Hyde of 'commercialization'. Yet both, of course, are aspects of Conservatism. It is as if it dare not cultivate in schools the intellectual qualities to understand the processes and sensibilities which it has been largely responsible for creating.

The strongest restrictions, however, on the development of the individual are those that arise from the anti-democratic nature of the Conservative programme, and from its fervent commitment to inequality. Every routine reference made by curriculum documents to an education that will 'enable people to participate effectively in a democracy' is offset by some practical measure that inhibits discussion of a controversial issue, or that curtails the exercise of a democratic right. Likewise, for every claim that the ERA opens opportunities, there is some new step in social policy that actively deprives the most disadvantaged people of the means which would enable their families to benefit from, or continue with, their education. So although the national curriculum is glowingly presented as an *entitlement* curriculum for all students, in practice there are many restrictions on such entitlement. The under-resourcing of education is the most evident, but for particular groups there are others equally disabling. At national level, there are no inducements for students from poor families to remain in education after 16: financially, they would be better off if they took a place on the Youth Training Scheme. The unemployed parents of school-age children will not find it possible, on an 1988 weekly income of about £70, to be able to meet the school's increasing requests for parental contributions, nor to provide the investment of time and energy that the slogan of parent empowerment demands. The obvious in these times needs restating: poverty is a great disenfranchizer; gross inequality cannot be the basis for democracy in education, nor for the development of an individual's potential.

Yet restrictions of this sort have not prevented 'democracy' and 'equal opportunity' from becoming central claims in the Conservative rhetoric of education. The basis of such a claim is set out in its most coherent form by Lord Young, who outlines the theories of knowledge that underpin the new education. Here, too, the weaknesses of the modernizers' case demands attention.

Modern Knowledge

In May 1984 David Young, head of the MSC and prime mover of TVEI was three months away from enoblement and Cabinet status. In that month, he gave the Haldane Memorial Lecture at Birkbeck College – *Knowing How and Knowing That: A Philosophy of the Vocational*. Education, he begins his lecture, 'has concentrated upon academic and intellectual pursuits to the detriment of the practical'. Academic education is based on 'intellectual operations'; it is 'primarily deductive'. Borrowing a term from the philosopher Gilbert Ryle, of whom he is apparently a follower, Young calls it 'knowing that'. He counterposes this kind of knowledge to 'knowing how' – 'intelligent practice', that embodies a knowledge that cannot be translated into the language of the intellect, and cannot be derived from it. The skier, the painter, the plumber and the entrepreneur all provide examples of 'knowing how'. Education undervalues it, and thus has a narrow conception of what constitutes intelligence. Young would widen the concept, to include not only qualities of artistic intelligence, but also those of being 'good at problem solving', 'highly practical', and 'good with one's hands'. Intrinsically, these are just as valid and important and desirable as knowing that. Young suggests, in fact, that on occasion they are more desirable. 'I sometimes dream', he confides, 'that if we lived in a world in which there was no Oxbridge and the highest from of academic establishment was the Slade School of Art, we would have different values. In that world we might well think of a painter as 'educated', even those who could draw or make things as able, and give scant consideration to those who could merely grasp academic concepts.'

Young, though, is not merely concerned with reordering the hierarchies of knowledge. His argument has a direct economic application. Democratizing knowledge is the key to modernization and competitiveness. The academic tradition in education was one of the reasons why, in the late nineteenth century, 'we lost our competitive edge'. Now, 'the gust of social change' makes it even more imperative that we have 'a working population both educated and trained, not just in the academic, the pure or the theoretical, but one with broadly based skills, able to adapt to change'. These skills will embrace several qualities – above all entrepreneurial ones. Large-scale industry is a thing of the past for Britain. Foreigners can do it more cheaply and more effectively. What is needed instead is 'a host of small companies, companies that will provide services... companies that will depend for their very existence on entrepreneurial skills, rapid development of products, customer service and a pragmatic and practical approach to life'.

This is the future, in which the development of the all-round personality and of the economy are perfectly synchronized. Towards the end of his talk, in a kind of visionary coda, Young attempts to draw together his philosophical and his economic themes. The labour market of the future will require schools to produce 'whole people', who will avoid narrow specialisms and who will be prepared 'for a world as yet unknown'. Their knowledge will not be narrowly academic. They will know how the democratic system works. They will know what private industry is about, and the 'importance, place and use of profits'. They will be able 'to fix washers on taps'; to 'prepare and paint a door'; to use 'a keyboard, a library or an electric drill'. Above all, rounding their personalities and attainments, they will be equipped with the lingua franca and the open sesame of the modern world. For, says Young, in an analogy which could serve as a memorial to the breadth and humanity of his vision, just as 'Latin was vital to the educated of the fourteenth century, so a knowledge of taxation and marketing is to the educated of the twenty-first century.'

Much can be said about the relation of Young's philosophy to his policies: between the theory of knowledge that he holds and the way it relates to the social order whose transformations he observes. First are the problems inherent in the sharpness of his distinction between 'knowing how' and 'knowing that'. Young imagines that the activity of an artist or a footballer is spontaneous and unreflective. It cannot be taught, and the principles which guide it cannot be fully expressed. When a footballer passes the ball, 'he just passes it there'. There is no time for concept formation: 'the thought is the action'. When an institute tries to teach aesthetic 'taste' – as in matters of town planning – environmental disaster follows. These propositions are dubious. In fact, within any 'knowing how' there is a 'knowing that', which can include – in the case of an athlete or a painter – a learned knowledge of technique, elements of deductive thinking, and a knowledge about the context of the activity. Each of these qualities is capable of being taught. A footballer can know from coaching and by deduction where the ball should go; a skier will need knowledge about weather conditions, and so on. The general point is that no activity, however 'practical', is as unreflective, as devoid of conceptual thinking, as Young would like to make it. As the pyschologist Vygotsky put it, all 'higher psychic functions', whose main features are reflection, awareness and deliberate control, are dependent not on motor reflexes, but on conceptual development, which in turn involves a development of language: 'signs are the basic means used to master and control them'. Young's expulsion of the conceptual from practical activity has particular, ultimately political, consequences.

Equally questionable are the issues that arise from his claim that, 'Knowing how is just as valid a form of intelligence as knowing that'. The historic downgrading of the first in favour of the second is not just a matter of the prejudices of intellectuals. Elite education gave preference to intellectual skills, including those of developed abstract thought, because they are essential to understanding and controlling natural and social forces. Countries and businesses are not run by those who possess practical intelligence alone. It is superficially democratic to preach the equivalence of the practical with the abstract – it seems to offer the possessors of practical skills equality with those trained in abstract thought. In reality, the argument serves

103

to crystallize existing social differences, by suggesting that there is no great need for those excluded by history and education from access to the linguistic tools of thought to make an effort to acquire them. And this is the stress of Young's argument: not to integrate 'practical' elements with an 'academic' education, but continually to suggest that a 'valid' education can be constructed around the principles of 'knowing how.' Antonio Gramsci, observing the practical turn of Italian mass education in the 1920's, understood the falsity of a prospectus like Young's. He criticized schools which were designed 'to satisfy immediate, practical interests', and noted behind their egalitarian, democratic watchwords a refusal to develop in students the capacity 'to reason, to think abstractedly and schematically while remaining able to plunge back from abstraction into real and immediate life, to see in each fact or datum what is general and what is particular, to distinguish the concept from the specific instance'. This refusal of the school, matched now by the direction of Young's argument, left access to the skills of reasoning open only to the already dominant social groups.

In Young's thought, the so called 'practical' (which in fact comprises the typical mental activity of millions of people) is severed in the sharpest of ways from the intellectual. This is especially significant in view of the way that he connects the narrowly-defined practical to the 'world of work', in such a way as to prevent 'abstract and schematic thought' from being brought to bear upon it. When John Dewey, most profound of progressive thinkers, argued for vocational education, he saw it as an activity which 'acknowledges the full intellectual and social meaning of a vocation', including 'instruction in the historic background of present conditions; training in science to give intelligence and initiative in dealing with material and agencies of production; and study of economics, civics and politics to bring the future worker into touch with the problems of the day and the various methods proposed for their improvement'. Politics, ethics and history were not extraneous to Dewey's concept of education, but integral to it. This is not the case with Young. In the appalling innocence of his claim that taxation and marketing are core aspects of a new renaissance in education, he lacks any serious consideration of the way industrial and commercial activities relate to human need. Thus the kind of change that Young advocates is far from being a democratization of school knowledge. In essence it endorses a narrowed concentration on the practical tasks involved in 'knowing how', at the expense of the issues which examination of the work process from a wider point of view can reveal.

Education, enterprise, equal opportunities

Young's arguments were not just the personal musings of a man soon to be Cabinet Minister. He was speaking as chair of the MSC, and his words reflected the essentials of its programme for educational change. The MSC, established by a Conservative government and set up in 1974 with full trade union support, had grown in influence during the 1970s. After initial suspicions of its corporate status ministers in Mrs Thatcher's government began to see it as a body with considerable potential. It became part of a general government effort to 'encourage an enterprise economy'. The Department of Employment, in describing its own work, shows how this economy is being constructed. Its first task is to promote the new growth sectors of the economy – such as small firms, self-employment and tourism. The second is to unleash market forces while weakening the power of unions to withstand them – or, as the Department more guardedly puts it, 'to help business grow and jobs to multiply by cutting red tape, improving industrial relations under the law by ensuring a fair balance and encouraging employee involvement'. The third is to 'improve training arrangements'. In the rhetoric of enterprise, these improvements involve providing high levels of skill and competence for all. 'The jobs of the future', says Kenneth Baker, 'will be upmarket jobs.'

An unravelling of the meanings of the Conservative programme can usefully begin with this last claim, that modernization necessitates higher skills and thus a better education for all. This is half the truth. The European TUC describes the major employment trends of the continent's economy as 'the creation of a small number of jobs requiring specialised training and high qualification; the elimination of many jobs on low and intermediate levels of skill; the lowering of skills required in many existing jobs'. The American heart of high technology, Silicon Valley, is itself, according to a journal of the American left, a land of 'two labor forces', as 'different in composition, wages and working conditions as if they belonged in two entirely separate industries'. While electronics engineers enjoy 'programmes and benefits that read like the entries in an encyclopedia of innovative workplace experience', for the production workers who make up half the industry, 'Silicon Valley means low-wage, dead-end jobs, unskilled tedious work and exposure to some of the most dangerous health hazards in all of American industry.' Others have pointed to the way these tendencies affect the British workforce. Against a background of incessant attacks on trade unionism – by law, by redundancy, by the media, by the loosening of health and safety and fair wage provision, by cuts in the social wage, an uneven modernization is taking place. In substantial ways, as miners, engineers, steelworkers have cause to know, it entails deindustrialization: the closure on a huge scale of uncompetitive or unprotected production. In others it involves growth: in the financial sector, and in high technology related industry. In the process, both areas have become more thoroughly integrated into international finance systems and divisions of labour. Around the successful large-scale enterprises, clusters of service and sub-contracting industries develop, some on the basis of self-employment, which increased greatly in and after the recession. This kind of modernization entails radically different experiences for different social groups. The areas of employment growth are, on the one hand, among 'managers, administrators, engineers, scientists and technicians'; and, on the other, in part-time, temporary or casual employment – low-paid work for which women are thought particularly suitable. These latter jobs could be in private services, in the public sector, or on the sub-contracting periphery of manufacturing, where workers can be hired or laid off according to the week-by-week requirements of the market. The demands of employers thus take two major forms. There is both a chronic, unsatisfied need for 'skilled, technical and craft workers', and a demand for casual and part-time employees who can spend the rest of their time on the fringes of the social security state. All sections of the workforce, however, will face a more volatile labour market, in which there is an increased possibility that they will be required to change jobs, develop flexibility, or, especially if they do not belong to the core of the workforce, adapt themselves to periods of unemployment. In a brief and less florid section of his lecture, Young had recognized this. He turned away from his vision of an entrepreneurial future, to make it plain that 'knowing how' has a special meaning for the less successful. 'Many, in our society of tomorrow', he said, 'whether they are true entrepreneurs or not, are going to have to take on responsibility for their own lives and economic welfare – to become more self-sufficient.' Responsibility in these cases involved acceptance of periods of unemployment and of periodic retraining.

It was against this background – of a process of modernization that was selective in its effects, but that was frequently mis-presented by an upmarket rhetoric – that the MSC was encouraged to increase the speed at which it changed from provider of special programmes to combat unemployment, to organizer of universal change in the employment and training of young people. A series of initiatives between 1981 and 1987 accelerated the transformation of the youth labour market and the training institutions associated with it. Jobs for young people virtually dried up. The apprenticeship system went into sharp decline. The 'Industrial Training Boards' which had been able to levy employers in order to fund skill training were for the most part abolished. In their place appeared a proliferation of programmes, at the centre of which were youth schemes of ever-increasing size. These programmes culminated in 1983 in the Youth Training Scheme (YTS) – designed to accommodate all jobless school-leavers. The claim was that YTS would provide a 'bridge between school and work', that linked work experience with training in a range of skills which would not be specific to any one job, but would be transferable across an 'occupational family'. YTS was intended to create a new kind of workforce, one that, in the words of Nigel Lawson, would have the 'right skills' and would be 'adaptable, reliable, motivated and prepared to work at wages that employers can afford to pay'. Sceptics disputed the first of Lawson's claims. Even assuming a two-tier economy, they said, YTS was not delivering either the quantity or the quality of training that regeneration required. The skill shortages which have become apparent in many sectors of the mid-1980s economic recovery bear out these criticisms, and indeed, were one of the reasons that Conservatives gave for winding up the MSC in 1988. Its functions were transferred to a new body, the Training Agency, that was even more clearly employer-led.

Other critics objected to the demands implied in the second part of Lawson's statement, at the same time recognizing their accuracy: the main function of YTS was to keep youth off the streets, while depressing its wages and job expectations. They also scrutinized the content of YTS, as they had done its predecessors. For an insufficient minority, perhaps, who had access to something resembling the old apprenticeship schemes, there would be good quality training. For the most part, however, YTS merely prepared large numbers of people for low-skilled, insecure employment. Its schemes concentrated on the inculcation of appropriate attitudes to work on 'social and communications skills'. One critic termed them 'skills training for deskilling, job preparation for unemployment'. They provided neither craft training, nor recognizable educational achievements, but concentrated on developing such qualities as 'motivation', 'self-esteem' and 'co-operativeness' – as if these nebulous achievements were of use to the trainee in the labour market, or educationally. Yet, for reasons which will by now not be surprising, the new line in training borrowed much from progressive education. The Social and Life Skills courses omnipresent in YTS were supposedly relevant to the everyday concerns of working-class youth, and their experience-based model of learning, that shunned most forms of explicit conceptualization, gained credence, as Andy Green has commented, 'through its apparent appropriateness to those who have demonstrated their aversion to academic teaching in the schools'. YTS, thus, was much more than a training scheme: it generated influential new models of education for a new kind of world of work.

It was on the basis of the growing educational sophistication of MSC programmes that, in 1982, Young had launched a 'Technical and Vocational Educational Initiative' at schools. Symbolically, its birth was announced not by the Education Secretary, who appears to have known little about it, but by the Prime Minister. The intention was to subject the school to the shock of outside, vocational influence, that could force the emergence of a new curriculum. The first response of educationists to TVEI was suspicion. They thought it would reinforce divisions in schools between academic and vocational streams; it was an unwelcome, centralizing intruder in a locally-administered school system; it would have more to do with job training than with general education.

Opinions soon changed, both because of the money the MSC could offer the selected 'pilot' areas and the progressive curriculum criteria that its National Steering Group devised. The existence of criteria, rather than set syllabuses, diminished fears of centralization, while ensuring a degree of conformity to general, MSC-set principles. They combined progressive with work-oriented themes. They pledged TVEI to developing 'equal opportunities for both sexes' – a commitment that has, as we shall see, been taken with some seriousness. Their learning objectives included, 'the encouraging of initiative, problem-solving abilities and other aspects of personal development'. To avoid one-sidedness, they specified that courses had to have a balance between general, technical and vocational elements, varying according to students' individual needs and the stages of the course, while relating technical and vocational elements to potential employment opportunities. Thus it became clear that TVEI would not be merely a school-based version of YTS: it would be better-funded and broader in its educational content. This shift in emphasis – which became more pronounced as TVEI developed – away from the 'vocational' towards the more educationally-acceptable 'technical' was not the result of some sudden change of heart at the MSC. It was rather the effect of pressure from the educational world, both from the top, among the education authorities which formulated individual schemes, and from the classroom teachers who had the work of devising projects and curricula. TVEI was assimilated within education, in a way that showed something of the detailed process of modernization: though the result of government initiative, it was not a simple imposition upon schools; the themes of the enterprise economy merged with the pre-existing interests of the schools, to form new types of curriculum. Critical assessment of the modernizing tendency must thus take into account not only the origins of the initiative, but also the way it changed at school level. Yet, for all this, it must not lose sight of the relationship between even the most progressive of modernising schemes, and the overall emphases of the enterprise economy.

Under the scheme, LEAs drew up proposals for school-based projects, in the main aimed at 14-16 year olds. Those which were approved by the National Steering Group were funded by the MSC and became subject to its regular evaluation. Beginning with 14 'pilot' areas in 1983, the scheme spread quickly. By 1985 74 out of the 104 LEAs in England and Wales were involved. Two years later it had become a 'national' scheme. In the process, it distanced itself from its explicitly vocational origins. By the middle of 1985, Lord Young could give it a new tone. It was 'not just about employable skills', but about 'educating people, about broadening the curriculum to give them new subjects to which to relate'. Within education, as one of its enthusiasts wrote, TVEI had become accepted as 'mainstream curricular reform with a long pedigree'. The educational press found that in several ways it echoed classic progressive practice.

> Young people of all abilities appreciate a more applied and vocational slant to their studies.... Many respond well to courses which break the conventional timetable mould, allowing whole days or half-days to be spent on project work or work experience.... The practical and technical are as highly valued as the academic .... Teacher/learner relationships are improved and changed.

Academic evaluations considered that it was 'eminently liberal and student-centred'. Pupils' responses 'almost without exception were extremely positive and favourable'. Teachers 'weighed in' to ensure that schemes were based on 'the comprehensive principle', with no growth of technical streams and no narrowing of educational experience.

The published syllabuses of local schemes, and the copious documentation the MSC supplies, allow some assessment of how TVEI's general principles worked out in local practice. It is possible to see in this process both the extent to which schools have modified TVEI's initial impetus, and the limits of that modification. Schools have moved away from the severely functional emphases of MSC philosopy while at the same time they have not sought to challenge its fundamental conceptions of the relation of learning to industry. The Hertfordshire scheme was one of the least equivocal about its industrial orientation. Its 'starting point' was an 'assessment of the skills and experience likely to be needed by industry and business locally and nationally'. It was decided that TVEI should include: 'industrial studies: how business functions in all its aspects'; computing and information technology; modern engineering design; electronics; modern office skills; 'an understanding of the manufacturing process from the identification of the need for a product, through its design, prototype, manufacture, testing, packaging and marketing phases'.

The much-studied Devon scheme is more liberal in its starting point. 'All TVEI students cover three areas of learning – technology at work, the world of business, personal and caring services.' Technology at work involves identifying a particular problem, finding and producing a technical solution to it, and evaluating the effectiveness of that solution. In the 'world of business', the technical aspects of production are complemented by study of the social relations it involves. Through first-hand experience – visits, interviews, research – students will come to understand business organization. They will find out about 'personal problems at work by interviewing adult workers about their jobs, by identifying an area of concern either from the management or the workers' point of view, and by investigating the work of the personnel department' and the counselling available to workers. Under the same heading, students will look at the role of finance institutions in relation to firms and individuals, discover the applications of modern technology in working life and 'explain the effects of local industry on the environment and community'. In the final part of the triad, 'the full range of study skills' is employed to learn about 'personal and caring services', that include 'community associations, domestic services, educational provision, facilities for the disabled, housing, recreation, libraries, religious and voluntary organisations', and so on. Alongside these courses are the by now familiar elements of an education for the new kind of individual: 'areas of personal study, such as coping strategies, self-presentation, deportment, grooming, diet, health, hygiene, safety and the use of household equipment'.

TVEI schemes combine, then, an orientation to the world of work with strategies for learning that emphasise relevance, inquiry and the use of modern technology. They make one further claim to progressivism: to be dealing with equal opportunity – especially in relation to gender – in a more radical and systematic way than any other initiative. It is not merely that TVEI incorporates aspects of the pedagogies of reform; it is also that under its aegis reform's objectives can be pursued with a new seriousness. The scheme sponsors a 'networking' of teachers, so that equal opportunity policies are not left as formal commitments, but are popularized and collectively developed. TVEI publications explain this concern in several ways. In philosophical terms, equal opportunity is a 'human right' which education should be promoting. More mundanely, 'in order to halt the decline in international competitiveness, the country needs to be able to harness the talents of all its people to their fullest extent'. There is a need for increased provision of certain types of female labour, some professional or technical, most casual and 'semi-skilled'. After all, most jobs that the economy has gained over the last ten years have been done part time, mainly by women, in areas like office work, tourism, leisure, catering, and so on.

TVEI's equal opportunity work centres on equality of access for girls to traditionally male subjects and jobs. Access can be made easier if role stereotyping is avoided, if positive role models are provided, and if the self-image of girls is strengthened. Teachers' attitudes have to be changed. Girls' interests must be seen as equal in status to those of boys. Boys themselves need to take seriously the conventional female areas of responsibility for families and parenthood. Outside the school, there must be a revaluation of the work women do. 'Only when women's jobs and qualities are valued equally with men's' will the character of life and learning change so as to make equal opportunities a vital principle.

If the principles of TVEI-in-practice are seriously to be challenged, it should be at this strong and provocative point of the scheme, where Conservative initiatives seem to have stimulated progressive methods and equal opportunity policies. Is it really the case that TVEI curricula give girls a fuller understanding of the part of work in their lives, and in this way empower them to press for change? Or is it rather that TVEI is still in essence a scheme trapped within the categories of Young's lecture, incapable of developing what Gramsci called 'abstract and schematic thinking', and of fulfilling the task that Dewey imposed on education, of 'bringing the future worker into touch with the problems of the day and the various methods proposed for their improvement'?

TVEI is in many respects an advance on the traditional curriculum. But, it still does not deliver, in any full and adequate sense, the kind of education that Dewey envisaged. Those who draft curricula that concern the world of work usually do so in the assumption that most things about it cannot be changed. Methods of production, for instance, and the human relations they embody are assumed to be fixed, pretty inescapably, by levels of technology and intensity of competition. As a result, school programmes of 'understanding industry' lack any sense that things could in any fundamental sense be organized otherwise, and thus lack also any rational standpoint for a critical perspective. Except, therefore, in some areas (such as those concerned with the environment) there is something tacitly monolithic about the knowledge of industry that such programmes generate. There have been alternatives. Among the most impressive was the Greater London Council's *London Industrial Strategy*, a volume that was simultaneously an account of the effects of Thatcherism on the economy of London and the lives of Londoners, and a set of strategies with which to oppose them. It covered almost the entire economy of Greater London, from home-working and the domestic economy, to engineering, office work, transport and the docks. In the GLC's approach, none of these areas of production was unproblematic, and each occurred within a context of social relations. Thus each involved conflicts and choices that concerned priorities, values and different ways of understanding. Out of these clashes came different policies for production:

> that of the manager is very different from that of the machine worker. The former is concerned with speed and control in order to increase profits, the latter with maintaining some control over how the job is done, with the use of skill to produce useful products, with a working life that enhances rather than degrades. There is also an

113

interest of users in the quality of products, in the overall balance between sectors, and between what is produced for sale on the market, and what requires an alternative public provision. At the moment over-riding priority is given to private market production and to the military sector, to increased intensity of work within the factory and the technological replacement of awkward labour. We can call this militarised market production. It represents the economics of capital. There is an alternative which we shall call socially useful production, which takes as its starting point not the priorities of the balance sheet, but the provision of work for all who wish it, in jobs that are geared to meeting social need. William Morris referred to it as useful work rather than useless toil. It represents the economics of labour.

The book then develops the terms of this dichotomy; it contrasts the redundancies, speed-ups, increases in casual and shift working, cuts and deindustrialization of monetarist London in the early 1980s with the possibilities offered by the city's human and material wealth for 'using wasted resources to meet needs' in a programme of modernization that serves the interests of people who live and work in London, in ways 'which involve them in the process of planning and restructuring'.

This 'economics of labour' is not only concerned with industrial production. 'For an economics geared to need, the household is the starting point.' The total time spent by Londoners – mostly women – in domestic work exceeds that spent in paid work. Yet it is usually regarded as outside the economy, and the social needs 'absorbed and hidden by the private labours of women' are rarely examined. The *Strategy* looks at what economic change is doing to domestic work, and the effects upon such work of new retail concentrations, of public sector closures, of cuts in health care and school welfare. It considers the effect on women's labour time of these changes, and concludes that 'if we calculated economy in terms of reducing all society's labour time, then cottage hospitals, local schools and better bus services would still be with us today, and all queues would be shorter'. It goes on to the ways in which the present organization of work in the home impinges upon the 'other half' of women's labour, their paid work. Here, though forty per cent of the London labourforce are women, 'careers, promotion, training and pay are still centred on full-time continuous working lives which allow nothing for the changing demands of responsibilities at home'. A strategy for this whole 'female' economy must set about a 'social reorganisation of labour', that accompanies positive action in the workplace, with extended public provision – of care, transport, and so on – that can make women's work less costly of effort and of time.

It is against this kind of understanding that TVEI can best be measured. To place the Hertfordshire scheme against the understanding of the work process set out in the GLC document is to grasp the difference between an approach that subjects work to questioning in the name of human interests and need, and one which places it entirely outside such interrogation. Nor is this merely a local error: it corresponds to the entire direction of Young's 'philosophy of the vocational', whose under-rating of abstract thought fails to equip students to inquire into the values and conflicts that are involved in any economic system. Even the more liberal Devon scheme, in its efforts to avoid too narrow a focus on employer need, reproduces the essential features of Youngian thought. It splits the world of work in two – 'technology' and 'business'. The first deals with technique, the second with some of the social relations involved in production – between workers and management, firms and communities. The problem is that these relationships are treated in a limited way. By suggesting, for instance, that counselling agencies or personnel departments should provide the main vantage points from which to observe the conflicts of work, the scheme reduces to an individual level problems of general significance, that could reveal much about the relations between groups involved in the production process. The progressive pedagogic methods of TVEI are thus not matched by a progressive social content.

Similar problems exist in the area of equal opportunities. The GLC *Strategy* sought to connect economic development with labour in the home. It understood the threads that link the status and conditions of working women to the burdens of domestic care. It registered the new demands that economic change places on both. In these ways, it tried to grasp some of the forces that pattern women's lives. Most TVEI schemes are not able to do this. Devon begins by separating the world of 'care' from the world of work, and thus is built upon a double weakness. First, issues of the quality of life are displaced from the sphere of production to that of personal services. Second, the separation hampers understanding of the way that women's work is spread across the two spheres. Correcting these weaknesses would entail re-ordering the way that TVEI sees and classifies the working world. At present, TVEI assumes that change in the economy means that employers have a vested interest in recruiting tens of thousands of women to well-paid, high-status jobs. There is little sign of this happening. As the GLC report stressed, women are being recruited to the periphery of the labourforce, to casual or part-time jobs. Others exist, wageless but with family responsibilities, outside the paid labourforce entirely. There is, in other words, a sexist division of labour which new developments in the economy reinforce rather than break down.

These processes in principle offer many learning opportunities. The focuses of inquiry could range from the details of the way individuals organise their working and domestic lives, to the greater and less obvious processes that both structure and change the lives of students' families and communities. Such inquiry would not centre only upon understanding processes, but on making judgements about them. In other words, it could meet Dewey's criteria for progressive education, in developing both an economic and an 'ethical' approach to vocational questions. The full range of progressive methods – first-hand investigation, interviewing, reflections on personal experience, independent use of resources – could be employed to develop that learning. Its relevance could hardly be called into question, and its value for the education of girls would be evident. But the characteristic curriculum of TVEI does not extend that far. The promise implicit in the joining together of progressive methods and 'real world' content is not fulfilled. Inquiry, in TVEI, has its limits. Yet, it must be stressed, there have been no better large-scale efforts to bring together education and the 'world of work'. Creative though the GLC's thinking was, it found no take-up in the educational world – not even in London, where the ILEA remained reluctant to encourage exploration of issues of production and of class. The integrated and imaginative vision of the London Industrial Strategy still awaits its educational counterpart.

116

4

All for the best?

The criticisms that the last chapter makes of Conservative policy are moral, philosophical, epistemological. They represent a response to the modernizing programme that is made in the name of a particular kind of humanism. The values they embody rest on ideas of justice, of equality, of democracy, of human potential. Cynics will already have noted that these criticisms are not, at least in any short-term sense, addressed to a more functional set of questions. Is the modernizing programme capable of contributing to economic growth? Will it strengthen Conservatism politically and ideologically? Will it achieve that thorough re-education of school students, parents and teachers that is necessary to right-wing modernization? If its policies could treat effectively the rot of centuries, and make British education an integral part of a programme that reversed economic decline, then opponents would be left only with the kind of critique that might be powerful on moral grounds, but that would have little practical impact on a successfully functioning system.

Conservative modernization claims to be bringing about such a system. The firm, creative hand of government fixes the outlines of educational strategy, while allowing a suitable place for teacher, and parent, initiative. Out of this matrix is emerging a curriculum that is genuinely an advance on earlier practice. It is broad: it gives science and technology the place long denied to them. It relates educational problems to the lives of students and the world outside the school. The links it encourages between school and industry make students see the usefulness of education, and help raise standards.

As well as being broader and more relevant, the new education is efficient. It specifies far more clearly than its predecessors the levels of attainment that students should reach. Through regular assessment of students, the work of schools can be carefully monitored. Standards will rise – but not by means of a return to a teacher-centred classroom, with student activities firmly controlled by the undemanding exercises of textbook and worksheet. The best of existing education has been assimilated to a new project, which is being pursued with a degree of will and organization previously missing. The Conservatives have done what the left could not, and harnessed educational energies to a coherent programme for national renewal, that at the same time provides the individual student with a sense of satisfaction and achievement. Modernization has become their property: they have worked for it.

The same apologists could argue that changes in educational control have likewise been beneficial. Though based, in the last analysis, on the decisions of the Secretary of State, the system allows full scope for consultation. Those associated with progressive traditions are not entirely excluded from the working groups which set out the detailed subject requirements of the national curriculum, and their influence, as in the Cox Report, has already been felt. Every working group report is circulated throughout education before it is agreed by the National Curriculum Council and, finally, by the Secretary of State. These are procedures which do not exclude the wisdom of the education profession, but which do subordinate it to overall policy requirements. Complementing the ultimate authority of the Secretary of State is a local system of school management that is more popular and less bureaucratic than that of the past. Parents' exercise of choice and their involvement on governing bodies will shape the education system, help control costs, determine patterns of growth and decline and establish the routines of accountability that will ensure teachers' delivery of a relevant curriculum. In this way, governing bodies will play their part in a grander scheme of educational financing, that will attempt to ensure that the cost of reform does not over-burden the economy. Instead of allowing a general expansion of educational spending, of the sort that so disfigured the budgets of the 1960s and 1970s, the government will target resources on particular priorities and will, if necessary, work with the private sector to do so.

These, then, are the claims that need to be weighed. Up to this point, of course, the writer has been wearing the mask of an apologist, in order to outline effectively the claims and achievements of the modernizing programme. It is a useful device, if also a dangerous one: the face can grow to fit the mask, in such a way that what is described can appear stronger and more coherent than it actually is, and critique be unwillingly transformed into a kind of grudging celebration. The mask, then, had better now be formally discarded: what follows is no longer a positive description but an assessment that focuses on the problems and contradictions of Conservative policy. Nevertheless, before it does so, it must register and explain, independently of any apologia, the extent of modernization's success, and the basis that has been laid for educational improvement.

This success is in its more obvious aspects political; the teaching unions' defeat is the plainest example. In other respects, such as the popularizing of beliefs that link low standards to left-wing influence, it relates not so much to the content of the curriculum as to ideologies about education. For opponents, these are the easiest achievements to acknowledge; they can be attributed to particular failings of strategy and presentation on the part of reform, and do not touch directly upon fundamental issues of content and control. In other respects, however, recognition of what Conservatives have achieved is a more painful matter. It involves accepting not only that the right has had gains presented to it by the maladroitness of its opponents, but also that its programme has already contributed in some ways to a raising of standards; and that its latest and most large-scale initiative, the national curriculum, is likely to lead to further advance, albeit of a sort marred by widening disparities of provision and attainment. Thus – it must be stressed – the claims made in defence of Conservative curriculum change have some basis in reality.

The list of effective, modernizing measures that have been taken since 1979 is by now quite a long one. It includes, most notably, the abolition of the dual system of examinations at 16-plus, and the establishment in 1986 of the GCSE. On the evidence of the first 'cohort' of students who have been through the new system, with its increased emphasis on coursework as much as final exam and its efforts to broaden the focus of its various subjects, results are considerably better than those of the

119

old system. Alongside this achievement exist others. Primary schools, for the first time, give consistent attention to science and technology. The TVEI is one of several school-industry projects that can claim to have stimulated new curricular approaches that amount to more than mere work-experience. And it is already plain from the initial documents of the national curriculum working parties that, if all schools were able to carry out their proposals, there would be a general rise in levels of attainment and breadth of knowledge. The primary English curriculum, for example, would include media studies and the use of information technology; some form of science education would be the right of all students.

Likewise, in the area of educational control, slogans of parental power have had an effect that cannot simply be described as reactionary. Though Conservative rhetoric is fundamentally consumerist, rather than democratic, it has served to put the issue of school-parent relations near the centre of educational debate and has led to legislation which increases parental involvement.

These features of policy do not give reason to modify the criticism of principles which was made in Chapter Three. They do, however, indicate why the Conservative programme can plausibly claim to have a modernizing impact, and why it has had potent political effect. Although often dismissed for its anachronism, its success has been built on an ability to continue, though in unexpected ways and with a pronounced right-wing inflection, the programme of modernization and democracy that reform announced on so many occasions in the post-war period, and yet was unable to deliver. Several recent historians of reform – David Hargreaves among them – have commented that this programme reorganized the structure of education, without reorganizing its content. The comprehensive school lacked a comprehensive, remodelled curriculum. One way of understanding Kenneth Baker's policies is to see them as an attempt to provide this unified curriculum for a mass education, and to respond to those awkward issues of the relation between school and community summed up in the phrase 'unpopular education.'

It is this element of continuation, of issues being pursued that were felt to be unresolved, yet present in, earlier approaches, that has made the Conservative programme surprisingly attractive to some educators. It is not that they have committed some great collective act of apostasy, but rather that they see in work around the national curriculum an effort to develop, and to establish in definitive terms, those attempts to renovate the curriculum that, in the 1960s and 1970s, met with only partial success. This element of *continuation*, and of the decisive resolution of questions previously recognized as important in other, non-right-wing discourses, is what explains the impact of the modernizing programme among educators, and what gives it a genuinely hegemonic status. It is hegemonic in the sense that it addresses the concerns of a wide range of social groupings and intellectual tendencies, beyond its immediate supporters, and wins their assent to a particular set of understandings and practical projects, even while they maintain, on other issues, a dissenting stand. It is hegemonic, too, in that it does not, on curriculum issues, seek to impose pre-set solutions, but is content to guide the broad outlines of the work done by those people whom it has recruited to its project.

To this writer, these advances are considerable ones. Linked to the development of strong constituencies of support among choice-orientated parents, they could create a Conservative hegemony, and a political base, at many levels of education. Yet, for all that, they remain in important respects at the level of potential, not realization, and stand in contradiction to other features of Conservative policy, which, under this government, are pursued with equal vigour.

The most fundamental claim of modernization is that it strengthens the links between education and the economy, and in doing so enhances the performance of both sectors. Yet despite all the changes it promotes, many structural failings of the British economy and education system remain, as untouched by the new strategies of Conservatism as they are unnoticed in right-wing diagnoses of decline. In its explanations of Britain's relative industrial weakness, the right has made great play with the alleged obstacles that the welfare state and public sector generally have placed in the way of economic development. It has neglected what, in historical terms, has been a much greater problem: the effect of the financial and overseas orientation of the British economy on its industrial strength. Investment overseas has been a huge drain on the 'internal' economy. The free trade policies which have dominated British economic history have enriched particular sectors, at the expense of industrial investment. In powerful defence of these policies exists a long-standing 'foreign trade' interest and a 'multinational' interest, which ensure that the voice of domestic industry is not a powerful one in the formation of national policy. The repeated failure of state and industry to adopt effective measures of modernization is related to this arrangement of interests, and to the fact that any forceful attempts to redirect investment to home-based industry would arouse the opposition of the commanding sectors. By contrast, Britain's competitors have been 'developmental states' that, with manufacturing interests to the fore, have planned and initiated strategies of industrial expansion. Conservative modernizers, however, seek all the gains of regeneration without attending to the inherent problems of a strategy that relies on the market to deliver that for which more powerful economies have planned. Thatcherism, with its disengagement of the state from many areas of economic activity, is in this respect a continuation in extreme form of long-established tendencies. From this perspective, several features of Conservative education and training policy fall into a pattern which signifies that the failings of the past have been resurrected in the programmes of the present. YTS, for instance, though much vaunted in advertising, is continually criticized for low standards of training. The MSC, having failed to resolve problems of labour supply, has been replaced by a body which throws on employers the responsibility for training – a job that in the past they have not carried out with success. The proportion of 17-year olds remaining in education, is, at forty per cent, less than half of German or Japanese proportions.

This pattern of inadequacy goes far beyond the requirements of a two-tier labour market. It is a systematic form of under investment that undermines all aspects of post-school education and training, from YTS to university. At school level, it is reflected in the contradictions of curriculum policy. In themselves, the documents approved by the National Curriculum Council are rational projects for educational development. They are undermined – not in any minor way but fundamentally – by failures of under-resourcing. To establish a properly functioning national curriculum would be expensive. Teachers need to be trained to operate it. They need time to prepare their work and monitor its results. There needs to be an adequate level of resources. The national curriculum documents assume the availability of staff, time and resources. In doing so, they are extravagantly optimistic. Schools do not possess the books or the technology to meet the demands that are now being placed on them. Teacher supply – as a direct and indirect result of government policy – is simply not adequate to meet national curriculum requirements. In particular subjects and regions a teacher shortage is now endemic. In late 1988, one London borough had only a quarter of its primary schools fully staffed. Other boroughs were in a similar position. There are specific, regional explanations for such shortages, that lie in housing costs and the strains of inner-city teaching. No such explanations suffice for the shortages of teachers in science, technology, maths and modern languages, nor the 'hidden shortage' of English teachers, many of whom are not specifically qualified for their work. It needs to be stressed that this problem is not at all accidental, nor short term. Throughout the 1980s government plans for teacher training numbers were pitched too low. Many of those trained never took up a teaching post – in the main because of low pay and the unattractiveness of teaching as a career. This latter perception, as we shall see, goes to the heart of the issues involved in Conservative change. The result of this chronic problem of teacher supply is that those teachers who are in post will not have the necessary time at their disposal to carry out the hundreds of tasks demanded by the national curriculum. A primary teacher, already in all probability lacking any preparation time at all, is expected to deliver nationally-specified curricula in English, science and maths, and to monitor and assess pupils – on top of the work she is presently doing. These features of the teacher's working life call into question the realism of the national curriculum proposals.

There are other ruinous strains that also arise from issues of funding. Over the next few years, the introduction of the poll tax and the ending of councils' power to determine a rate to levy on local businesses will further restrict their ability to raise revenue. The proportion of council funding coming from central government will rise to seventy-five per cent, and will not be generously provided. In this process, it is the inner-cities which will be particularly affected. Already, councils preparing to take over the functions of the abolished ILEA have been told to prepare for several years of further reductions, so that by the mid-1990s spending will be twenty per cent lower than in 1989. Those Labour councils which attempted in previous years to maintain high levels of spending, faced with threats of bankruptcy and legal action, have made very large cuts in resources and staffing. From one point of view, these developments could be seen as perfect illustrations of a two-tier policy: the rundown of locally-controlled, non-selective education will enhance the attractiveness of new selective systems, and grant-maintained schools, or City Technology Colleges, will come into their own. In reality, such a smooth process of sorting out is unlikely to occur. The devastation of inner-city education by consistent policies of underfunding will create strains that are likely to find forceful political expression. Conservative policies are likely to face continual challenge from students, parents and teachers. In the context of the general under-resourcing of education, the forcefulness of inner-city protest movements could, given suitable political conditions, link up with expressions of concern from other parts of the country to create a powerful challenge to the whole direction of government policy. The Conservative hope is that self-help and making-do will come forward as alternatives to protest about resources. The question is, whether making-do will be typical of the national picture, or whether encouraging parental involvement at a time of continued restrictions on resources will produce even more vigorous protests than those of the early 1980s, as parents, better acquainted with budgetary issues, demand more money for their schools. If this happens in any consistent way, then the notions of parent responsibility that the government hopes will dominate the agenda will occupy only a secondary place. Classical issues of equal opportunity politics, related to resources, will resurface in powerful ways.

Financial issues are likely to be at the root of future discontent. They will not, though, be the only sources of agitation. Other strains will be created by the conflict between the profound authoritarianism of the Conservative programme, and its claims to be the Education of the Future. The modernized curriculum stresses qualities of initiative and problem-solving on the part of the student, and requires that the teacher be more active too. The systems of national testing, for instance, will not require so much the marking of the students' written product, as the evaluation of the way that s/he has gone about a task; thus the teacher will need to be more closely involved in observing, and intervening in, the processes of learning. This model of the active teacher – with what could be called a higher level of educational culture – is in conflict with every other Conservative policy for the teaching force. At each point in teachers' working lives they encounter the effects of an authoritarian politics, that has spread through government initiative into every corner of the system: one thinks of the primary headteachers who, imposing Baker's conditions to the letter, require their staff to remain on the school premises for half an hour at the end of the day, even though there may be no work for them to do or meetings to attend. Nor do pressures like this stop at the classroom door. What they teach is placed under greater surveillance, and new restrictions are placed upon it. If they stray too close to controversial issues, they can expect to live in fear of press disclosure. If a school strays from the national curriculum, the law gives parents the facility to report it to the Secretary of State. Within a few years, teachers will face compulsory annual assessment of their work. Behind the slogan of accountability is occuring a process which drains away from teachers a sense of involvement in and responsibility for their own work. Yet it is these teachers upon whose commitment the implementation of the national curriculum relies. It is an open question whether this commitment will be given, or whether there will be a 'performance strike' in which it will be invisibly, but potently, withheld.

A further problem of the Conservative project concerns the tensions between its different strands. There are many features of new rightism – especially of the cultural kind – which are ill-at-ease with a modernizing project. Most fundamentally, there is an unhappiness with the very condition of modernity and its attendant pressure for constant change and re-adaptation. Marenbon prays that politicians may observe a 'chasteness towards fashion'. Beattie complains that 'much is sacrificed to the gods of change and fashion' and Honeyford states with some relief that 'it is now intellectually respectable to question modernism in all its guises'. 'Cheap commercialism' is bracketed with 'Marxist relativism' as a threat to the 'culture of society'.

Such views could be understood, perhaps, as reactions to the leftist leanings of modernism as a cultural movement, if it were not for an aspect of new right thought that strikes at the heart of any modernizing project – that is, its rejection of 'relevance' as a curricular principle. 'Education', Scruton writes, 'is a kind of extended war against relevance.' The demand for relevance interrupts education's own spontaneous order, which has been created over centuries by the free flow of interest through autonomous institutions. These interests have not been shaped by immediately relevant concerns. If they had been, they would not be of educational value, for it is by pursuing the apparently irrelevant that education confers its lasting benefits, and brings students understanding of the human condition by enabling them to stand back from it. The position is held too widely to be a personal idiosyncracy of Scruton. 'The idea', writes Oliver Letwin, former adviser to the Prime Minister on education, 'that a school's aim is to train people for jobs is noxious.' Schooling is 'on a par with, not subservient to, economic work'. Frank Palmer, editor of a book on *Anti-Racism: an Assault on Education and Value*, takes the point further, into an attack on the whole pedagogy associated with vocationally-orientated change. His charges could equally have come from the humanist left. 'The twin cries' now are for 'skills and socialization'. 'The concept of a "person" is immolated .... Many of our educational managers ... extend an open-armed welcome to the resurrected behaviourist', with no conception of 'fundamental and complex human capacities'.

Behind these views, as we have seen, is more than just an intellectual position. They express the complex make-up of the dominant culture of England, the lowly status of industrial interests within the British power bloc, and the difficulties they have in elaborating social and cultural ideologies that would assist a project of modernization. For not the least remarkable thing about Letwin's ideas is that they are published – along with a number of other pamphlets of a similar tendency – by the Centre for Policy Studies, that think tank which draws it funds

126

from some of the largest industrial companies. It is surely a sign of an important weakness that industry can do no better than allow the views of a Letwin to crown the work of one of its best-funded pressure groups. There is no 'modernizing' think tank equivalent in weight to the CPS. There are plenty of industrial liaison projects, which have their effect on the work of the school, but there is no organization, representing industrial interests, that tries to develop a programme for curriculum modernization, that can be publicly made and strenuously lobbied for. The tendency, as expressed through the funding given to CPS and the other pressure groups, has been for 'industry' to allow its role to be usurped by organizations which, though they may provide effective means of undermining political opponents, are quite irrational in the programme they draw up for schools.

Their attitudes are dismissed by those who see central direction – and an assault upon what Barnett attacks as the 'English' concept of 'the self adjusting anarchy of autonomous interests' – as the only means of regeneration. Yet they are stronger as an influence on policy than they have been for many years, and they grip the imagination of a large section of the Tory Party in the most tenacious of ways. Pro-business the Conservatives may be, but that does not prevent their seduction by themes that, though rich in talk of traditional standards and of cultural identity, constitute no more, in terms of any modernizing project, than a series of false trails. The right is continuing to use its substantial influence with sections of the Conservative Party to press for a simplification of the national assessment system, so that there will be simple pen-and-paper tests, with the student's mark compared to a national average. Thus testing would not become a means of increasing the pace of curriculum modernisation, but rather of holding back that development, so that the traditional and easily measurable skills of the past would maintain their grip on the schools. Likewise, the concern to preserve sixth form education in its traditional ways has led to the retention of the 'A' Level system, at the expense of a broader set of courses, that might offer more chance of combining sciences with arts, the academic with the technical. Successful amendments to the ERA, designed to promote Christianity in schools, require an expansion of religious education, and an increase in the number of RE teachers – hardly an efficient use of resources at a time when modernization is already making huge demands of them. Opting out contains a similar combination of unwanted financial costs and dubious political consequences. In its first months of operation, it had the effect of keeping open schools which local authorities, acting at the behest of a government which wants to eliminate 'surplus' school places, had decided to close: hardly, from a Conservative viewpoint, the most efficient use of resources. In the longer term, opting out will be a vehicle for the right's hostility to the centralizing tendencies of the ERA. The goal will be to increase the school's autonomy, in the confidence that, pursuing its own interest within a framework of minimal state-set standards, it will evolve a curriculum that, by reproducing the features of tradition, will meet parent demand. Over the next few years, pressures of this sort are not likely to die down – yet they are antithetical to the conclusions drawn by modernizers from their study of British education, that educational development requires central intervention, a curriculum that does not turn its back upon modernity, and a judicious assimilation of suitable parts of the progressive tradition.

Placed thus in the context of a government policy which is forceful in its regulation of political life and its control of ideas, yet has an ineffective record of economic intervention, the modernizing programme becomes less imposing. Rather than the all-powerful, dynamic heart of Conservative policy, it appears instead as one of a number of competing influences; its effectiveness is constrained by factors that are by no means only short-term consequences of financial austerity, but have deep roots in the authoritarianism of Conservative rule, and in the hegemony exercised in political and cultural life by non-industrial influences. The future of the Conservative politics of education will be marked by continuing internal conflict, that is likely to be intensified by the protests of teachers and parents against the effects of central aspects of its programme. But to indicate the probability of conflict is not to assume the collapse of the whole project. The opponents of Thatcherism will not be able to take full advantage of the tensions within it unless they possess convincing strategies and programmes of their own.

The next two chapters examine the possibility of such alternatives, first by considering the responses of the historic proponents of reform – especially the Labour Party – to Conservative change, and then by setting out a programme for education that has a chance of matching the Conservatives for popular appeal, while defending a very different set of values.

5

Responses of reform

So far, the main focus of this book has been upon the ideas and the achievements of the right. In this treatment educational reformers and radicals have figured largely as targets: their work has been viewed from the perspective of their opponents – glimpsed through the sights of Conservative weaponry. From now on, the focus changes. The right is still a looming presence in these next two chapters – the extent of its success makes that inevitable. But the main questions that the chapters pose are now no longer concerned with explaining the scope and future potential of the Conservative programme, but with responses that are being, or could be, made to it.

The starting point for these explorations is the striking weakness of the political response to the Education Reform Act. The ERA overturned most of the principles by which reform has stood. It introduced testing, encouraged selection and racial segregation and undermined local authority control of schools. Almost every comment that the world of education made about it was negative. Yet it passed through Parliament with very little fuss. The major changes to the original Bill – to reinforce the Christian character of religious education, and to abolish the ILEA – came from the right, not the left. This could partly be explained by the size of the Conservative majority, but the weakness of other types of response to the Bill could not. Despite the thousands of critical commentaries that were written, there was no effective campaigning activity against it. No co-ordinating committee linked together opponents of the Bill; there were no token strikes, no demonstrations. Remembering its successful campaigns for 'educational advance' in the 1960s, the NUT booked the Albert Hall for a rally in defence of education. Full twenty-five years ago, in 1988 the Hall was two-thirds empty. That its response should be of this kind – rich in words and poor in actions – reveals much about the present difficulties of reform. It signifies both the real difficulties of mobilizing support and the will-sapping assumption that, however much campaigning work is done, popular backing will remain elusive. In one way, this hesitancy is a tribute to the success of the right, and to the demoralization created by the vigour and scope of its changes. However, beyond the immediate effects of the right's activity, the response to the ERA reveals a deeper kind of failure.

In crucial respects, the programme of reformers was inadequate to their proclaimed goal of providing a high level of education for all. Patterns of opportunity and of educational achievement had been little altered by the coming of the comprehensive. It was true that there had been a steady improvement in exam results, though many researchers questioned whether this was due to the new school system. What was undeniable was that success in academic terms was confined to a narrow layer. Beyond the academic level, though the new secondary and primary schools were undoubtedly pleasanter places for students to be, there was still a persistent undervaluing and misunderstanding of students' experiences and culture, of such a kind that allowed the comprehensives' most eloquent and supportive critic, David Hargreaves, to write of the assault they perpetrated on students' sense of dignity. It was this system for which reform took responsibility, at first with pride, later more defensively. Increasingly, it was taking responsibility for failure, without possessing the ideas that could build on the non-selective virtues of the comprehensive system, and develop a new education programme that would be more determined in its attacks on privilege and more radical in its conceptions of a relevant curriculum.

Throughout the 1960s and 1970s there was an attempt, in the name of progressive education, to reform the comprehensive curriculum. But progressivism, though it correctly stated the importance of building educational development upon the interests and motivation of the individual, did not sufficiently consider issues of curriculum content. Stressing 'discovery', 'relevance' and 'expression', it downplayed the enormity of the task of equipping non-privileged students with the knowledge and conceptual equipment they would need to improve their life-chances, still less to understand and change their world.

131

Progressivism, moreover, expressed in a heightened way all that was sectoral about educational reform. It was adroit in establishing an influence at certain points within the education system, but less attentive to seeking support outside it. In popular terms it was more likely to be the butt of criticism, rather than a rallying point of campaigns for change.

These, then, were some of the long-standing problems of reform. To them should now be added the effects of the Conservative onslaught, which has exposed long-standing weaknesses to harsh new tests. Almost all the forces which once led the pressure for reform, whether for comprehensive education or for curriculum development, have been subjected not only to a barrage of criticism but to a series of practical measures that has weakened their influence, broken up their unity and made it difficult for them to carry out even their most basic functions. The main teaching unions have lost members, councils have had their finances cut, and locally-generated curriculum reform has come almost to a standstill.

Yet their journey to this present slough of despond was not pre-ordained, nor has it taken the form of a smooth and regular descent. At particular moments, it has seemed possible that there will be a vigorous counter-offensive. At the beginning of 1985, for instance – nearly six years and two elections into the period of Conservative rule – it was possible to survey the educational scene and conclude that in several ways opposition to government policy was stronger than ever. Teachers' unions were on the point of launching what the NUT's General Secretary later called the 'longest dispute in the history of public education', over salaries. Local councils were preparing what they said would be strong resistance, backed by union action, against new laws on rate-capping that limited the revenue they could raise from rates. On curriculum issues, several Labour-controlled LEAs had begun to work out radical and detailed policies for dealing with inequalities of race and gender. It could not be said that education was a conquered city, nor, against the background of the miners' strike and the public support it evoked, that Conservative policy in general enjoyed unchallenged ascendancy.

Two years later, all had changed. The counter-offensive was over, and the government, and the right, had won. The following sections describe the nature of the reforming challenge, and try to explain the instrinic weaknesses that lessened its chances of success.

The teachers' action

By early 1987, after tens of thousands of days of strike action, and the investment of the hopes and energies of the larger part of their membership, the main teaching unions were facing the consequences of failure. Their attritional campaign had cost the Tories Keith Joseph; it had lost the largest TUC-affiliated unions thousands of members, and defeat had intensified the internal divisions in the NUT. In staffrooms, there were all the usual varied after-effects of failure: anger at a leadership which in many eyes had made important, premature and demoralizing concessions of principle, cynicism about the value of being a union member, relief that the strains of action were over, powerless resentment at the new duties that the Pay and Conditions Act heaped upon teachers. In many areas, there was a sense that those who had been most active in the strikes had written off their chances of promotion. Alongside this mood of irritated quiescence, sat those who had done well from the defeat: the headteaching and non-TUC unions, whose members, with varying degrees of pride, had not taken action, and now experienced the sweetness of unchallenged power or the salaried rewards of industrial inactivity.

In some eyes, the action was doomed from the start. The government had just beaten the miners. It had clear plans for dealing with teachers. The teachers themselves were divided: six different unions, two of them representing school managements and one founded on an anti-strike platform; the two largest and most militant locked into an unending membership war, and the third, the 'Assistant Masters and Mistresses Association' (AMMA), building itself on the basis of recruiting the less militant members of the larger unions. The government, said one parents' leader, would have the teachers for breakfast. Many teacher activists, less vocally, held the same opinion.

In these circumstances, it must be asked not only why the teachers' campaign was defeated, but why the action began at all, and what sustained it for so long. At one level, it was given impetus by the experience of teaching in a new climate – a feeling that schools were under-resourced and that teachers' workloads and management demands were alike increasing. At another, the campaign was fuelled by anger at the way teachers were being held responsible for crises in diverse areas of national life, from the economy to the family, and from sporting failure to football violence. In general, the action can be read as a response of teachers to what they saw as a devaluing – literal and metaphorical – of their work, as part of a process of social change whose animating ideas were for many antithetical to what inspired their teaching.

Like much intense trade union activity, the union action was also a way of affirming the possibility of a different way of doing things. The refusal to cover for absent teachers, for instance, established a degree of teachers' control over an important aspect of their working lives, that also brought the evident benefit of a reduced workload. The action embodied different kinds of relationship among teachers, that were based on consent and solidarity rather than the commanding managerial authority which many saw as a tendency that, government-supported, was growing in strength. Yet this central feature of the action, that helped sustain it for so long, was hard to communicate to those outside the school – especially as it was not connected to an approach to educational problems of a general kind.

The teachers' action related to the wider politics of education in a number of ways. Its own politics were both implicit and limiting. Its motivations may have been complex and far-reaching, but its explicit programme was much narrower. As one supportive critic from the Black Parents' Movement noted, organized teachers were 'weak on issues which were not about pay and salary structure'. Although the wider funding of public education was a constant theme, the unions had not made it a consistent campaigning priority. Still less was the momentum of the campaign employed to raise wider, non-financial questions of education policy. Thus, although their action represented an intensity of militant effort previously unparalleled among teachers in England and Wales, its positive long-term effects were few. The militancy *within* the largest unions found few counterparts in purposeful alliances outside, with parents, or other trade unions, or political parties. In fact, though it is hard to write, the effect of the action was to deepen public scepticism about the capabilities of teachers. The impact of the strikes was enough to force the government on to the defensive, and to raise questions about the funding of education, but was not sufficient to generate new thinking about 'standards' and educational purpose. These were issues that remained in government hands. The action over, campaigning parents' organizations in some areas continued their work; but on the whole the high tide of militancy left little behind as a basis for opposition to the Conservative education programme which, after the strikes, swiftly took shape. To some extent, the action had even narrowed down the interests of teachers. For some years they had refused to be involved in after-school meetings, and had thus in effect withdrawn from curriculum development. For many, this was not just an 'industrial' sanction: it expressed an attitude to new demands placed upon them by government and LEA initiatives with which they had little sympathy. For some of those already disenchanted with change from above, the 'withdrawal of good-will' sanctioned by union action set the seal on a private disengagement from curriculum development. In future, after the action, they might attend meetings, but their fuller commitments would be elsewhere. Justifiable though it was, however, this loss of heart in many of those who had previously been involved in 'grassroots' curriculum change increased the influence of the centre. Under Baker's new conditions, the meetings and extra days set aside for curriculum development gave LEAs and headteachers the opportunity to transmit the latest official thinking to teachers, among whom were many who were not so much convinced of the overwhelming virtues of the new policies, as doubtful of their own ability to resist the workload they implied – still less to find support for alternative curricular views. Gradually this complex process of resistance and accommodation is draining the pool of ideas and initiatives from which alternatives to the dominant policies might eventually come.

Councils and teachers

Meanwhile, there had also been changes on other fronts. By autumn 1986, the ability of local councils to construct little bastions of municipal socialism amid the advance of Conservative policy had also ceased to be credible. The collapse of resistance to rate-capping and the exhaustion of the possibilities of creative accounting now faced councils with their only remaining option: to save money by making large cuts in the workforce. In 1987 and 1988, the one-time big spenders of local education – Labour councils such as ILEA, Brent, Haringey, Manchester, Newcastle – planned cuts in jobs that led in several cases to confrontations with their teachers. ILEA, in these two years, compulsorily redeployed more than 2000 of its teachers, while offering golden handshakes to hundreds more. In 1988 Haringey, threatening redundancies, provoked a six-week strike by NUT members that prevented sackings and achieved a partial defence of conditions but could not stop the loss of hundreds of jobs. Brent, a latecomer to massive cuts, made up for its tardiness later that year, by giving short notice of the loss of more than 200 teacher jobs. In the events and arguments that surrounded these measures there became evident the hostility that Labour councillors had built up, over the long period of pay action, towards the NUT. Blaming the teachers' action for the voters' loss of faith in Labour and in state education, they turned with some relish on the local union branches, and showed themselves obdurate in negotiations. Aggressive management attitudes, about which teachers had long complained, were suddenly intensified. 'Casual' teachers were laid off. Redeployment had the effect of breaking up schools as working communities, and of targeting particular, militant teachers for movement. The effect of these new attacks upon teachers who were already experiencing wholesale media rubbishing of their work, as well as the pressures of social crisis and 'innovation overload', was to deepen attitudes of alienation. In their hundreds, teachers applied for the voluntary redundancy schemes which ILEA, Brent and Haringey put on offer. So many quit that a problem of surplus quickly became one of shortage. In staffrooms, reactions to these developments varied from apathy to rage: none were conducive to the development of further progressive reform.

Local curriculum reform

With the defeat of teacher militancy and the intense, government-induced conflicts between teachers and the vanguard of reforming LEAs, the different elements of the progressive bloc were fast fragmenting But these were not the only areas of difficulty. The events in Brent, referred to in Chapter 1, demonstrate in a particularly vivid and compressed way other sorts of tension within the bloc, and the way in which they provided opportunities for the right. The significance of Brent, however, does not only lie in the ruinous clashes between teachers and LEA that occurred there. From another point of view, the initiatives of the local authority had something in common with the teachers' campaign on pay and conditions. In each case, there was a response to educational crisis and inadequacy, which took the form of a break from tradition: extended periods of militancy on the one hand, determined action to transform the school's relationship to black students on the other. But in each case too, the focus on a single feature of the education system proved inadequate. Just as the teachers' campaign was weakened by an inability to link basic issues of working life to wider questions of performance and purpose, so the Brent initiative ran into trouble at the point where it could be made to appear a project which was dealing with one aspect of equality, at the expense of the interests of other students. This was not the only line of attack levelled at Brent, but nevertheless it was an important one. Media demagogues were able to fuel fears that white students were locked into a zero-sum competition with blacks, in which measures to reduce black inequality acted to the disadvantage of whites.

The infamous Development Programme for Race Equality was a well-planned initiative to deal with low achievement by the black majority in the authority's schools. It aimed to reshape the curriculum and working practices of schools, 'so as to improve the attainment and life chances of pupils'. The changes for which it worked would be thorough-going: it would develop curriculum content so that 'the experience and identity of all students' – not only whites – would be 'affirmed and valued'; styles of teaching would be rethought; the 'involvement of ethnic minority parents' in the school would be increased.

To achieve these objectives, the programme established senior teacher posts in every secondary school, with the intention that those who held them would co-ordinate race equality initiatives and make them an integral part of the whole work of the school. In addition it established project teams, to work in depth in small groups of schools, so as to develop – for instance – pre-school education, secondary humanities or school-community relations. They would aim to build on existing good practice, develop it, and popularize it among teachers.

Some idea of the projected work can be gained from the brief of the secondary 'Language, Literacy and Literature' project team. It would

> foster and extend the linguistic diversity and skills of pupils; involve study of the range of literature and reading materials produced by black writers ... promote the development of writing abilities across a range of forms and for a variety of audiences and purposes; create greater opportunities for pupil talk and the development of conceptual abilities through talk; recognise the value of bilingualism ... foster language studies ... and make available to pupils the opinions, literature, talk and writings of other pupils and of adults in the wider community.

Thus the most productive recent thought about linguistic and intellectual development was linked to a project of race equality. The attempt was eminently justifiable in educational terms: it linked school-based learning to 'real-life' experience; it was attentive to a diversity of cultures; without losing sight of literacy issues, it envisaged a widening of the the way that language and literacy were treated in the curriculum.

This was not the way the press saw it. For the *Mail on Sunday* DPRE was an authoritarian imposition on teachers, that tried also to enlist black students as footsoldiers of an educational adventure that aimed to 'bring our democratic society crashing down around our bourgeois ears'. It was all right to give 'extra help' to ethnic minority students as 'low attainers'; it was quite another thing to reshape the whole practice of schools in order to combat racial 'inequality'. This was an intrinsically totalitarian attempt to stamp out the school's natural way of doing things, that would lead to more cases like that of Maureen McGoldrick, and a permanently 'Orwellian' atmosphere in schools.

This became the dominant interpretation of DPRE – or, at least, it was the interpretation of the dominators. Agreeing with the *Mail* that something had to be done, the government set up an inquiry into Brent's use of the Home Office 'Section 11' money which had funded DPRE, and specifically investigated DPRE itself. Unsurprisingly, new and more restricted criteria were established for the use of funding, so that, for instance, anti-sexist education would not be part of its brief. DPRE itself was allowed to survive, provided that Brent agreed to place it under the overall supervision of a committee headed by none other than Baroness Cox.

The whole incident, in one sense, was just another example of the symbiosis of tabloid press, government initiative and right-wing pressure in the slandering and subsequent neutralization of potential radical challenge. Behind the noting of the blatant exercise of power, though, exists another more awkward issue. Could DPRE have been more effectively organized and defended, and did its difficulties reflect overall weaknesses in the project of reform? One answer to these questions has already been given. Necessary and, in some senses, exemplary though it was, Brent's setting up of DPRE still suffered from a sectoralism that allowed space for its own outflanking: the right could pose as the defender of all those disadvantaged students whom DPRE did not address, and for whom Brent did not seem to have such a detailed concern.

But this was not the only problem. To plan and carry out radical initiatives is a test not only of the skill of programme devisers. It is also a test of the culture of reform – the way that crises are managed, potentially antagonistic groupings reconciled, and individuals encouraged to take a positive attitude to change. It thus puts to the test entire administrations, and the apparatuses which they control. Here Brent failed, in ways which the bureaucratic mishandling of the McGoldrick case illustrated most vividly. It lacked the political skills that would have allowed it to escape the 'totalitarian' allegations that filled the *Mail on Sunday*; on the contrary the McGoldrick case only

139

increased their plausibility. In this context, absurdly enough, DPRE could be presented as a clamping down on classroom initiative, rather than an attempt to roll away the great weight of monocultural uniformity which had pressed down upon the students in Brent's schools.

Lastly, local initiatives, in order to survive, need to breathe the air of national support. They need to be surrounded, justified and defended by a discourse which can present ideas simply and attractively and respond in a sharp and effective way to criticism. In the case of DPRE, as with other initiatives concerning race equality, that climate was missing. Although willing to speak up in favour of 'multi-ethnic education', the Labour Party did not spring to the defence of anti-racist initiatives. When the right discovered some instance of a student writing an anti-racist poem, or a school holding an assembly on Mandela, or a teacher pinning up a poster on aboriginal rights – all incidents which made the national press in 1987-8 – Labour did not manage a forthright defence. It would not have been difficult. Forceful words on the pervasiveness of racism in British institutions, or loud praise for the liberation of schools from the stultifying grip of a conformist culture would at least have begun to challenge the right, and to impede their steady capture of race as their own issue. As it was, efforts to extent equal opportunity concluded in debacles for which the national leadership of the Labour Party must take some of the blame.

Drawing a balance-sheet: Labour

The difficulties and tensions within education allowed a new surge of right-wing agitation, that capitalized on the work of nearly twenty years. Its effects were not total: popular campaigning against the abolition of the ILEA indicated, amid all the intense conflict over its cut-back policy, a strong reserve of support. Likewise, in the middle of the Haringey strike – which provoked some parents to petitions of complaint against teachers – other parents demonstrated their support, some to the extent of occupying a classroom in a school from which a teaching post had been removed. Experiences of this kind of militant defensiveness were many. Nevertheless, the last two decades had taken a toll. The notorieties of progressive education; the 'extremism' of curriculum reform; the inefficiency of Labour local government; the continuing problems of comprehensive education – these themes had been worked on tirelessly, with a wealth of detail, by media for which education had been one of the running scandals of the whole period. They were not pure fiction – if they had been their effect would have been less – but rather interpretations that framed and linked up a collection of diverse and real experiences of education. Strikes, reform in controversial areas, school student protest were the realities of the period; it was the achievement of the right to have constructed a set of ways of seeing those experiences which interpreted them, not as signs of experiment, vitality or righteous anger, but as the noxious products of a worldview that combined naivety about the limits of the possible with intolerance towards those who dissented from it. Drama and anecdote were as important as research to the construction of these interpretations. Newspaper accounts of particular stupidities and abuses linked up with 'independent' studies and the specially commissioned reports of the inspectorate to provide a densely detailed 'map' of education that guided, and was to various degress absorbed by, common sense. In this the right had achieved one of its great successes and had attained what Honeyford wished for it. In substantial ways it had written the language in which the experience of education could be expressed. It had grown from sectional origins to aspire, credibly, to a universal status. In doing so, it had entered regions where previously the local language had been one of reform.

It was out of these experiences – of setbacks and of the underpinning sense that an entire system and strategy of reform had been exhausted – that Labour came to rethink both its interpretation of what had happened in education, and its own programme for the sector. In doing so, it was forced to come to terms with the success of the right: a process which brought Labour to the edge of what had once been the unthinkable. It was one thing to argue that the weaknesses of reform had presented the right with specific, and skilfully-used, opportunities for agitation. Much of Labour's rethinking, however, went further. It was not only that the right had been able to exploit weaknesses – but that in certain respects its programme addressed uncomfortable truths about the nature of education which Labour had for too long avoided. Perhaps the disruptions of the teachers' campaign, the failure of standards to rise much above those obtained in the old selective system, and the continual row about indoctrination were less the effects of underfunding or media invention than the expression of trends that had grown strong during the period of reform and now encouraged the pursuit of intellectual fads and sectoral interests at the expense of standards and efficiency. Perhaps, therefore, the Tories were right, and parental demand was a sounder basis for constructing an education policy than producer interest.

It is 'existential' questions like these, which raise fundamental doubts about the entire reforming project, that are involved in Labour's rethinking of its education policy, and are operative in the measures advocated by some of its leaders in local government. Questions of this type, though, do not arise solely from developments within education. The present shape of Labour's education policy cannot be understood without reference to the steady revision of platform and presentation that Labour's leadership believes is necessary to win an election after ten or a dozen years of Conservative rule: the celebrated new realism. The 'conditions of possibility' of new realism are the defeats suffered by militant trade unionism and by the left in the party, whose enthusiasms are blamed for the scale of the last two electoral disasters. It is far more however than a tactical realignment of platform: its rethinking has developed, unevenly and often in piecemeal ways, to extend to a range of strategic and philosophical issues which bear directly on present and future education policy. At its base it is possible to detect three related beliefs: one about the nature of contemporary capitalism; the second about the nature of a possible British socialism; the last about the means and agency of social change.

The first belief accepts the predominant role of the market, and asserts it vehemently against those who, gaining ground in the 1970s, had advocated planning and large-scale state intervention in the economy. Its adherents hold that the changes that stem from the recent operations of the market system – internationalization of production, shift of investment away from smokestack industries, changes in the composition of the workforce – are unstoppable and not necessarily malign. They have created a new social landscape, a basis for beliefs and attitudes vastly different from those of the past, to which Labour must adapt if it is to survive. Older models of Labourism rested upon the support of the masses of workers in large-scale industry, and built up the huge collective institutions of health, housing, education and social security. They must now give way to newer models that recognize the break-up of collective identities which has occurred with the run down of traditional industry and the moves towards diversity of provision within, or outside, the welfare state. Contemporary society is distinguished by greater diversity of production; and consumption, too, no longer follows fairly uniform patterns. People are more aware of themselves as consumers, rather than clients of the state or members of the collectivities of workplace and community. Solidarity, equality, struggle are less significant concepts than individual freedom and choice.

Connected to these understandings is a second set of beliefs. Socialism is not after all about social control of the economy or transformation of its purposes. It has instead to do with limited intervention to regulate the more blatant dysfunctions of the market system and to ensure that its fruits are more equitably distributed. On top of these rather traditional tasks, there is Labour's duty to develop a programme of what the Shadow Cabinet minister Bryan Gould calls a 'socialist modernization' appropriate to the new era. Politically, it should stress individual rights; economically, it should search for new means of giving employees a 'stake in the productive process'.

Out of these positions comes a serenity about a properly- run capitalism's ability to satisfy basic wants. There is also a marked lack of interest in areas quite recently highlighted as central by other currents in socialist thought. The *London Industrial Strategy* examined the kinds of relationship between people that occur in economic activity, the quality of life that they embody and the wider social effects that particular systems of production create. Now the focus has shifted. Unsatisfied need, stifled aspiration, structural inequalities and oppressions – these are not recognized within new realist thought.

The third major element of new realism is its conception of how social change will be brought about. Neither the struggles of the traditional core sectors of the trade unions, nor the new social movements have the weight to trouble Conservatism. In

143

fact, the opposite is true: in as much as they offend the burgeoning middle layers of society, they are actually counter-productive. Any organization that employs forceful collective action, or that pursues controversial issues, is thus liable to be treated coolly.

The alternative model links up Labour's thinking about agency with its ideas about the kind of future that is desirable and possible. It envisages change carried out by governments and councils that do not reflect union struggles or turbulent movements for qualitative change, but rather implement a programme of moderate reform that is much more sensitive than the Labourism of the past to the views and pressures of non-union constituencies, and that wins electoral success by forsaking too close an involvement with producer groups. Particularly in the public sector, there is a new interest in the rights of the consumer, who is no longer to be the powerless client of a bureaucratic apparatus, but will be given rights of information, consultation and choice. Likewise, there will be a new priority given to serving the consumer well, through managerial efficiency. Labour's 'over-riding objective has to be to guarantee the quality of the outcome of the services', as a paper prepared for one of its Policy Review groups puts it. Undoubtedly, there are ways in which this reshaping of purpose would correct some long-term problems of the remoteness and inefficiency of public services. In others, though, it is deficient, to an extent which would compromise any programme of qualitative change and disable even the limited reforms aimed at by the new realists. The concentration on what could be called a quantitative efficiency begs the question of the criteria on which this efficiency is based: it does not, in other words, pose questions of need and purpose. In the same way, the abstract and universal term 'consumer' serves to conceal the divergent interests and demands of different social groups. Both 'efficiency' and 'consumer' are conceptual vacuums, likely to be filled, in the absence of questioning, by the conventions of present middle-ground thinking. The turn away from producer interests deprives reform of potentially its best organized and most informed social base, and makes its programme even more vulnerable to the pressures of the better organized consumer groups.

Flourishing among new realism, then, are ideas that are evidently full of implications for education policy. From them spring explanations of past weaknesses, new interests in standards, efficiency and the consumer, and new models for relations between the different parties involved in schooling. They are being developed in the shadow of Conservative success, and embedded in them is an acceptance of many features of the world as it has come to be during the Thatcher years. But they have not changed everything. It is as foolish to pretend that Labour has abandoned an interest in improving social provision as it would be to claim that new realism is the intruding serpent in an Eden of socialist thought, whose scheming will lose us paradise. In some respects, it is no more than an updated but selective development of powerful elements in the Labour tradition – which, after all, has been better known for an accent on some greater degree of fairness than for a commitment to social transformation.

Thus, in education, there is a retention of certain elements in the 'equal opportunity' tradition. This had always been an area of unresolved ambiguity. Was education related to individual need or manpower planning? Was 'opportunity' a matter of trawling the ocean of working- class talent in order to find new candidates for expanding layers of the workforce, or was it a means of empowering groups to achieve what Labour's 1974 manifesto, in a memorable but short-lived burst of radicalism, called 'a fundamental and irreversible shift in the balance of wealth and power to working people and their families'. In general, the more economically-orientated arguments had prevailed, but there persisted under Labour – especially in the 1960s and 1970s – a dynamic that had pulled reform in other directions. Research projects probed the limits of comprehensive reform as a strategy for raising the levels of achievement – and the occupational success – of working- class students. Teachers and lecturers pointed to the irrelevance of much of the school curriculum to the experience and interests of those who endured it. There flourished for a time currents that denounced the school as an agency that socialized and graded the future workforce. It was not that these themes were ever dominant at high levels of policy-making, but that the way education had developed – professionally rather than politically directed,

145

locally-improvised rather than centrally controlled, in a climate of reform marked also by the growth of critical theories of society – created a permanent 'opening to the left'.

It was this dynamic, or drift, that had elicited Labour's most famous contribution to the education policy of the 1970s. In 1976, in a speech at Ruskin College (location, once, of a celebrated struggle for an independent working-class education) James Callaghan had sought to ensure that educational development was firmly centred on new national priorities, while its more radical tendencies, labelled as failures, were suppressed. 'Let me repeat', he had said – presenting the conventional wisdom of the DES as the latest word in Labour policy – 'some of the fields that need study because they cause concern. 1/ There are the methods and aims of informal instruction. 2/ The strong case for a so-called core curriculum. 3/ What is the proper way of monitoring the use of resources to maintain a proper national standard of performance? 4/ What is the role of the inspectorate in relation to national standards and their maintenance? 5/ And is there a need to improve relations between industry and education?'

In several ways, Callaghan prefigured Labour's later policies – perhaps most importantly in the particular vantage point he constructed. Essentially, it combined two sorts of grievance: those concerned with 'national efficiency', as it is imagined by dominant social groups, and those much more inchoate complaints, that in some way reform has failed to meet the needs of the mass of people for a more relevant, more engaging, more beneficial education. The central point about Callaghan's speech – and about so much Labour rhetoric since – is that it *acknowledged* the second set of grievances, but *articulated* only the first. The sense of unmet aspirations was present but, as it were, occluded, written over by the available and confident script of the argument about efficiency. Discontent, then and now, has found no readier set of terms in which to explore and experience, or to describe how things might differently be done.

The effect of Callaghan's speech was both immediate and long-lasting. He succeeded in embedding in Labour's thinking ideas profoundly critical of reform. He accepted, for instance, that there was in schools a problem that could be analysed by reference to the term 'standards'. In this contention were brought together popular grievance and high-level policy. It ran like an underground stream through Labour's policy of the next eleven years, invisibly mining the foundations of its confidence in state education and those who worked in it, to surface, spectacularly, in 1987 in the spouts of calculating anguish about the performance of state education that marked post-election rethinking. Most immediately, though, it was his final question that affected Labour's policy For the next decade it was to have at its centre 'education for the world of work'. It was this that became the filter through which equal opportunity was understood. The basic assumption – pre-existing new realism – was that the imperatives of economic change marched in the same direction as those of human need. To this extent, Labour's ideas corresponded to vocationalism. The distinctive Labour contribution was to qualify this acceptance in two ways. First, by linking economic growth to social justice: the key to economic vitality lies in reducing selection and elitism. Second, by complementing the student's economic understanding with moral and creative qualities. Uniting the two themes, Neil Kinnock argued that education policy must change, 'if the country is to be fit for the future as an industrially competitive, culturally fulfilled and socially just society'. In both cases, however, the principles of justice, creativity and so on are weakened by an assumption that the social relations that arise in the course of work are not for changing. Kinnock's epithets are there to show that Labour has, in the words of its one time educational spokesman, Giles Radice, 'a more generous, less narrowly vocational vision of education than the Tories'. But, in a manoeuvre that has its counterpart in vocationalism itself, they 'add on' the creative or the personal dimension to an idea of vocational education that accepts the logic of a particular economic system. The whole person comprises the ideal worker *plus* the concerned, creative citizen. There is no sense, in this vision, that its elements may be in tension – that the demands of work and those of the creative personality may not fit easily together. To assume that they do, and to link unquestioningly justice with efficiency is in fact to set limits to Labour's policy. Efficiency, defined always from a particular dominant viewpoint, takes priority. Measures of equality can be taken; access can be promoted at every level from nursery to post-16. But while the

147

content of education is derived from the most conventional ideas of purpose, it is difficult to see how Labour's programme can substantially embody the principles of fulfilment and social morality that trip from Neil Kinnock's tongue.

Labour has drawn upon equal opportunity in response to the two-nation model of modernization. In doing so, it has expressed some sense of the value of education in terms broader than the economic. Something more is needed, however, if it is to take up other potent areas of the programme of the right – and many politicians of the new realism are willing to recognize that. Contained in Labour's current discourse, therefore, are themes of culture and individuality that draw from, and in some important respects revise, the party's traditional social thought. It is in these areas, especially the second, that new realism makes its most significant contribution.

The right's foregrounding of cultural themes has revealed the poverty of Labour's thinking, especially in areas where new social movements centring on issues of race and gender have posed questions about national identity and family life that the party has not cared to handle. The shyness of its leaders in responding to the the legal bans on the 'promotion of homosexuality' is notorious. 'Labour has never sought to promote homosexuality', was the first response of its leadership. Its inability to get beyond the platitudes of multi-cultural education to discuss issues of racism in British culture is likewise remarkable. What, then, of Labour's traditional strength – its concern for 'working-class people'? Can that perhaps be a basis for responding to the right on issues of culture?

Class, in some ways, has never been absent from Labour's thinking: as a divisive force that restricts economic growth; as a collection of disadvantages that handicap individual development; as unwarranted privilege whose existence affronts the principles of social justice. In these senses, it serves as a kind of shorthand for the possession or lack of cultural capital or material wealth. It enters state education as a force for which the school should compensate, something whose effects working-class students should be encouraged to overcome. These aspects of class are not illusory and for many they are all too real. The problem is that for Labour they completely take the place of other understandings. The most important of these, in an educational context, is that 'class' can designate a set of relations that helps to structure the lives, experiences, ideas and identities of large groups of people. In this latter understanding, class is given an affective depth that deprivation theory can never match, while at the same time it has an explanatory function, in conceptualizing the forces and conflicts which give experiences some of their pattern. Neither of these elements is present in high-level Labour thinking, which still treats class as a synonym for deprivation. Even in progressive LEAs, in their brief mid-1980s heyday, class was a difficult issue – the subject, as we shall see, either of conventional treatment or of silence. Thus when the right began to organize the educational agenda around issues of culture and identity, Labour was hard put to reply in terms that related to the experience of its constituency. Since it did not aspire to the felt-in-the-bone nationalism of the right, and did not explore the possibilities of class-related alternatives, it could muster only a weak response to the cultural dimension of Conservatism. It tended to borrow some of the older phrases from the repertoire of its opponents, and to counterpose them to the 'divisive' approaches of the right. Jack Straw, opening the debate for Labour on the Education Reform Bill, praised the more emollient figures of Conservative tradition:

> Butler was a one-nation Tory, a worthy successor to Benjamin Disraeli whom the Secretary of State quoted. Butler recognised that it was only through equality of opportunity that talents could flower, that richness and diversity in our national life could occur, that individuals could be fulfilled and that one nation could be created.

Earlier, as if to underline that his use of 'one nation' did not only signal a desire for a consensual education policy but extended also to cultural issues, Straw had accepted the principle of a national curriculum, on the specific grounds of cultural unity. 'There's a common culture, so we have a core curriculum.' The individual richness and diversity to which Straw referred in the House of Commons are not, thus, the outcome of cultural conflict and struggles against the dominant meanings, so much as the fruits of a broad and tolerant consensus.

There are similar problems with Labour's interest in the individual. Bryan Gould wished to restore 'individuality' to Labour's vocabulary. 'We have somehow persuaded ourselves', he wrote, 'that the only identifiably socialist virtues are those which can be expressed at a high level of generality, and that socialism is brought to a full stop as soon as it is a matter of individual people actually becoming better off. Yet if we cannot deliver to real, identifiable people, what is the use of our policy?' At this level, the argument has value. It is on the brink of addressing the complexities that motivate social action and political motivation. It is when Gould comes closer to specifying how he understands the nature of these 'real, identifiable individuals' that the thinness and lack of complexity that afflicts Labour's view of class – and of social identity generally – again becomes plain. 'We have to appeal,' he said in another article,'to the individuals who own their own house, a car and perhaps £500 of shares.' Individuals here, as Hilary Wainwright has pointed out, are 'real and identifiable' in terms of the property they own. This is not a negligible factor, but to isolate it means that the various social relationships – gender, occupation, family histories and so on – which give identity its complex and shifting nature are simplified out of existence. He does, though, give a further hint about the make-up of his target group. Labour's history disposes it to suspect 'the values of those who are not disadvantaged' and it is thus cut off from a potential political constituency. It is time to learn that there is nothing intrinsically wrong with privilege and the values that arise from it, but their exclusivity. 'The most effective attack on privilege is to spread its advantages to everybody.' For a realist, this seems an unusually innocent position to hold: semantically absurd, economically – from Gould's position – unlikely. Yet it is significant none the less. If he wished to designate an egalitarian policy, it was open to him, as to socialists of the past, to use some phrase like 'equal shares in the wealth of society'. He prefers to talk in a different way, to draw attention to the values that arise from relatively privileged social positions, and to suggest that Labour's programme should take them more seriously into account. But what is entailed in present-day privilege? Thatcherism has worked to establish a relationship between wealth, the way wealth is accrued, and the social attitudes and political dispositions of individuals. Share-ownership in privatized companies, gains on the property market, private health insurance, even the pay rises of workers in a union whose collective powers have been weakened and which resorts to direct mailing and postal ballots to involve its members – these are not merely material improvements in the lives of some people, but changes that bring with them altered outlooks and values. Outside of private lives – contained more than ever before in small family units, yet 'mobile' as never before in the opportunities available, selectively, to them · continues a decline of the public sphere, both in the sense of the involvement of individuals in the social and political life of their society, and in the sense of the breaking up of institutions that exercised a degree of social control over the processes of economic life In reality, there is no 'privilege' that is abstractable from these processes; and to pursue such a quality is a kind of adaptation to the Conservative achievement. Yet it is along this path that much of Labour's discourse about policy is now moving.

Neil Fletcher

The most dramatic shift in discourse and policy formation, though, is not that embodied in Labour's Policy Review, but in the arguments that emerge from the leader's office of England's largest education authority – Inner London. The novel feature of Neil Fletcher's ideas is not just that they assume that Labours need a change in programme to enable it to cope with the new society that Thatcherism is helping to create, but rather that they take up and apply to Labour's educational policy several of the criticisms made by the cultural right. They do so, moreover, in ways which are especially marked by a disenchantment with the work of teachers. Fletcher, more than any other Labour politician – at least in public – registers this disenchantment, and seeks to deprive teachers' organizations of the positions of influence they once enjoyed within the reforming bloc.

In 1982, the ILEA symbolized for the right everything it hated in state education. Neil Fletcher, its future leader, then a councillor in Camden, was regarded by the left-wing *Labour Briefing* magazine as someone 'committed to (try to) administer

151

an arm of the state in more radical fashion'. By 1987 Fletcher, now leader of ILEA and chair of the Association of Metropolitan Authorities' Education Committee, had become a byword among Conservatives for his apparent acceptance of their educational critique, and among London teachers for a confrontational style of management that seemed to value neither their commitment nor their jobs. In these shifts is captured something of the 'moment' of new realism – the pressures that have shaped it and the political choices it embodies.

Three kinds of experience are crystallized in the arguments that Fletcher developed in the autumn of 1987, and for which he sought wide publicity. The first is that of the teachers' militancy, seen from the perspective of the Labour local authorities. The second, and least explicit, is the experience of LEA-led radical reform of the curriculum. The third is the incessant pressure of the right, and the inability of the progressive bloc to hold it back.

He argues that there exists a basic 'consensus in favour of comprehensive education' and a widespread belief that each local community should offer a good quality, adequately resourced education for all children free at the point of need'. The Education Reform Bill is a deadly threat to these principles. In itself it is a 'tawdry collection of measures', which nevertheless has a gained a certain credibility. This it owes to its ability 'to mine a vein of parental and public dissatisfaction with schools'. Its assiduous sapping of belief in the comprehensive system, though, has passed Labour by. 'The party's presentation of its ideas on education has been disastrous.' It has explained the problems of education purely in financial terms, and confined itself to 'routine denunciations of Tory demonology' that simply don't 'pass muster for an alternative strategy'. It has understood neither that questions of 'organisation, curriculum, philosophy, ethos, accessibility and accountability' are central to education policy nor that reforms need, not just money, but 'the political and organisational will to implement'. As a result, it has failed to halt the underachievement persistently deriving from factors of race, class and gender. It is time that Labour dealt with these areas, and in the process re-appropriated the 'vital concepts of "standards", "achievement", "quality" and "choice" that the Tories have made their own'.

Thus far Fletcher illustrates the strengths of new realism.

Borrowing from the critiques developed by the radical left in the 1970s, he recognizes that it is the weaknesses of reform that have given the right its opportunity, and dismisses the kind of economism that led Giles Radice to claim that the trouble with the Tories was that they didn't make education a priority! Fletcher realizes that something has to change, that old ideas can't relate to the present situation, and that questions of content and control will be crucial to developing an effective Labour policy. It is at this point, when it comes to specifying what these questions mean in practice, that the problems start.

Fletcher suggests that comprehensive education 'as currently provided does not stretch ... children enough or provide them with the essential skills needed for survival in the modern world'. Children's special talents are not being developed. The 'move away from rote learning' is in danger of 'deskilling a generation'. Working-class children are still not doing as well as their middle-class peers. Teachers underestimate the potential of children from ethnic minorities. Girls continue to be excluded, in effect, from science and technology in the upper secondary school. Too few students stay on after 16. Parents, in too many cases are 'still treated as lepers' by heads and teachers. To put matters more forcefully,

> comprehensives, new teaching methods and modern aids were failing working class children who were massively under-achieving. If new teaching methods are not delivering the goods to working class kids they must be looked at and ultimately rejected.... Excellence should be at the centre of our programme along with opportunity and peace.

There are several accurate observations of the problems and misdeeds of comprehensive education here; but they are set within a framework of interpretation which is ultimately both conservative and ineffective. Fletcher, like the right, organizes his argument around a counter-position of 'excellence' to 'modern teaching methods'. Every time he touches upon concrete issues of teaching and learning, he finds himself endorsing by implication the methods of the past, which have been so noticeably unsuccessful in raising overall levels of achievement among working-class students. He dresses up the more conventional forms of educational practice and presents

153

them as solutions to the problems of the underachievement of working-class, female and black students. 'He called', reported *The Teacher* in December 1987, 'for a return to traditional teaching such as memorising verse, saying such activities are the basis of academic success.' It is not an impressive argument. So long as ideas like this are the practical content of terms like 'standards' and 'quality', then the attempt to claim the rhetoric of excellence from the Conservatives will resemble the effects of the Trojans' take-over of the Wooden Horse. The 'vital concepts' of the opposition infiltrate to the heart of Labour's discourse, disabling it politically and preventing the development of an education relevant to its constituencies.

The problem is deepened by Fletcher's understanding of equal opportunity. For classical Labourism equal opportunity was an attempt to give working-class students a better chance of getting the jobs previously available only to more privileged groups. It was a matter of providing different personnel for a division of labour that itself remained unchanged. In reality, the chase after levels of working- class achievement sufficient to oust other classes from their occupational positions was utterly chimeric. Equal opportunity of this sort was thus no more than a means of levering up a relatively small number, which grew as a result of the expansion of white collar layers of the workforce in the 1960s, but which never reached the point where the boardroom, the Inns of Court and the officers' mess were peopled by the products of the comprehensive system.

Fletcher, however, believes, 'in his heart of hearts that the purpose of comprehensive education is to ensure that working class children do better than the rest'. When this purpose is linked to his traditional conceptions of educational content, Fletcher is making literally impossible demands of the school. He is asking it, employing unchanged models of education, to overcome the effects of the basic inequalities of society. The result of such demands can only be the creation of a new spiral of disillusionment about the work of schools, as they fail to surmount what he calls the 'excuse' of socio-economic background. This is not to say that the only alternative to his ideas is a kind of revolutionary fatalism which holds that nothing will change for the good in schools unless the social relations that exist around them are transformed first. Schools can promote an education that highlights and opposes social inequalities, investigates how the world and lives of students have come to be what they are, and considers what might be done to change them. In this context, it is possible to imagine an education that raises 'levels of achievement' in many forms, while not being guided only by the star of examination and career success. This requires, though, a general change in the way that learning is organized and the objectives that are set for it. Fletcher's speeches and writings, which contain behind their rhetoric of equality an acceptance that schools prepare students for a 'reality' that, unquestioned, can only reflect the demands of dominant groups, do not envisage such a change. Yet, a few years earlier, ILEA had, under a different leader, in certain respects begun to explore it.

In 1981, for instance, ILEA began to consult minority ethnic groups about questions of 'school achievement'. In this process, 'the black communities made it clear that they wish for an unequivocally anti-racist policy'. As part of its justification for such a policy ILEA argued, in the manner that so outraged Roger Scruton, that racism is 'all-pervasive'. It affects all 'interpretations of human behaviour, literature, the arts, habits, conventions etc.'. Consequently, 'the system of knowledge, the curriculum, media, books and learning resources that have been developed in this country present negative, stereotypical and distorted images of black people and other ethnic minorities'. The precise merits of this analysis – which will be touched on later – are less important here than its critical stance, and its insistence that, in order to deal with underachievement, what schools teach and the way they teach it require fundamental change. For black students, a 'better' education has to be an education of a qualitatively different kind: it is not a question of taking older models and applying them to all. For Neil Fletcher, on the other hand, the dimensions of anti-racism have shrunk to a question of 'under-expectation'. The views of 'black parents' are translated simply as a demand for 'better', rather than 'better and different'.

Fletcher is at his most aggressive in dealing with the people who will have to implement change. Out of the experience of conflict with the most militant section of teachers in the country – the Inner London Teachers Association – he denounces teacher trade unionism more strongly than any Labour politician for decades. 'We have bent the knee too readily to the teaching unions', he writes. Parental tolerance with their 'antics' has worn thin. They must stop their strikes, accept their new, imposed conditions (described as 'a new flexibility and additional challenges') and develop a 'strategy to restore public and parental confidence in their professionalism'. On this basis, 'unity' between them and the Labour Party may be restored.

He has in mind a unity in which teachers know their place. The accent is not on a joint effort by organized teachers and the Labour Party to develop a new education policy. It is rather a matter of teachers accepting their auxiliary – albeit, under Labour, better-paid role – in a process of change that relies on the existing, post-Baker management structures to regenerate the whole process of teaching and learning. His stress falls upon the role of 'the most talented heads', the 'innovative curriculum managers', the 'expert teachers'. Change is a management issue. There is no sense that the commitment and energies of the rank-and- file of the teaching force are crucial to change. The focus of his interest shifts to 'parents', a concept in which are brought together several of the themes of new realist thought. The appeal to parents is recognized as a key factor in Conservative success. Labour must match it – listening to grievances, entering debate, providing information, offering choice. 'After all', says Fletcher, underlining the consumer motif, 'isn't that just what the private sector is so confident that it does?'

In as much as Fletcher is pointing here to the need to gain popular support, his argument is valid, and several of his specific proposals (open access for parents to schools, for instance) would be part of any programme for school democracy. The problems, as always with new realist appeals to the consumer, lie elsewhere. 'Parents', in Fletcher's construction, have several different functions. They are a mechanism to hold in check the activities of the producers – though, in contrast to the new right, this would be done more through debate and through consultative structures than through quasi-market pressures. More significantly, the concept is used to assert that there exists a single, unified parental constituency, in which differences of race or class or political attitude produce no important variations in need or viewpoint. This tendency to merge interests into one undifferentiated whole in practice strengthens everything that is 'non-political' and conventional in educational provision and discussions about it: universality is usually the discourse in which specific needs are dissolved. Finally, the concept, in the way it is used as the only indicator of a non-teaching, non-LEA interest in education has the effect of completely filling up the space that might otherwise be allocated to a diversity of interests – school students, community organizations and trade unions – so that the needs that education might serve are glimpsed only from a partial viewpoint.

For all the weaknesses of his case, Fletcher's ideas are of interest because they take account of the difficulties of reform and the success of the right, and try to develop new policies to deal with them. The attempt involves rethinking matters of content and pedagogy, and reconsidering the agencies and alliances that can lead to change. His thought is thus broad in scope, but is still too much contained within the framework of new realism, and of the unreconstructed ideas of Labour's dominant traditions, to offer an effective alternative. There has, however, been another detailed and cogent attempt to rethink these questions, that also begins by looking in an unflinching way at the weaknesses – catastrophes, even – of particular reforming strategies, yet goes on to develop a serious and practical radicalism that makes no concessions to the right.

Burnage

It is a rethinking that arises from a death. Ahmed Iqbal Ullah, 13 years old, was murdered in the playground of Burnage High School, in Manchester, on 17th September 1986. His killer was a white schoolmate, Darren Coulburn, also aged 13.

It was not the first savagery at Burnage High School. In January 1982, 'the son of the Deputy High Commissioner for Bangladesh, who is based in Manchester, was attacked by five fellow-students in a totally unprovoked incident, and received serious facial injuries including a fractured cheekbone'. The school and LEA at that time 'blindly denied the existence of a racial element in the violence'. The memory of this incident, and the long catalogue of less dramatic everyday abuse that continued in the years up to Ahmed's death, meant that the Asian community, school students included, reacted in bitter concert to his killing. His family 'pledged that his death should not be in vain'. An Ahmed Ullah Memorial Committee was set up. As a result of its efforts a committee of inquiry was set up by Manchester City Council. Unusually, in the world of education, its report was not written largely by whites. Three out of the four members of the inquiry team were from ethnic minorities. Their combined experience reflected two decades of ethnic minority campaigning against racism in schools.

The report seeks the causes of Ahmed Ullah's death. It looks for them not only in the mind of Darren Coulburn, but in the policies and culture of Burnage High School, and the wider influences that have gone into their making. It is very detailed, not only in the sense of gathering a wealth of empirical information, but in that it is attentive to the complexities of Burnage. It gave a picture of a school which was not attentive to the needs of its white working-class students and whose all-male intake facilitated a culture of aggression that only the recent appointment of some women teachers had done something to mitigate. It depicted a racism deeply embedded among some teachers and students. These failings and brutalities did not 'dominate all social relations at the school', nor were they 'fixed and unchangeable'. Nevertheless, they had created a knot of problems which only the most subtle and resolute of strategies could have resolved. Into this context came a new senior management that was committed to anti-racist policies 'in perhaps a more whole-hearted way than any other Manchester school'. Yet its policies, the report concludes, inflamed rather than resolved the tensions of the school.

At this point it would have been easy for the report to take refuge in discussion of managerial efficiency. It does make judgements of this sort – but in a way that seeks to account for mistakes by searching out the policies and beliefs that underlie them. Anti-racism of the kind practised at Burnage is thus subjected to theoretical scrutiny. This was the exercise that so excited the press – another anti-racist council laid low, this time by the criticisms of black investigators. Uniquely among recent criticisms of reform, however, this one was made from the left. The 'theoretical model' of anti-racism applied at the school was criticized because it placed racism 'in some kind of a moral vacuum, totally divorced from the more complex reality of human relations in the classroom, playground or community'. In this kind of anti-racism, 'there is no room for issues of class, sex, age or size'. Moreover it assumes that 'white students are all to be seen as 'racist', whether they are ferret-eyed fascists or committed anti-racists'. White people were kept out of the fight against racism, whether by the exclusion of white parents from groups set up to develop anti-racist education, or by the ban on white students attending the funeral of Ahmed Ullah. In these ways, the model had 'added fuel to the fire of racism' and had led to 'a polarisation between black and white students and to a potential escalation of racial conflict'.

The report suggests a different strategy against racism, and in the process also rethinks questions of working-class education. Anti-racism is best developed in the context of a policy attentive to the needs of all disadvantaged groups. From this perspective the policies of Manchester City Council are criticized. The council turned down the suggestion of one of its working parties, that it should develop a policy on 'class discrimination,' 'since it was felt that this issue was too controversial'. To omit class, says the report, 'means that the council's policies will not be addressing the grievances of the white working class majority, meaning that their interests as a group are nowhere catered for'. As a result, the 'practitioners and theoreticians of the white backlash' can have a field day. The report itself does not make this mistake. It tries to explain the views of parents involved in this backlash, by relating them, not to an innate racism, but to an entire historical experience, in which the school has played its part. 'After hearing the evidence of the Parents English Education Rights group ... one gets the sense of white working class parents who have little basis on which to root their own identity, and whose education has given them little or no conception of the value of their own experience as English working class.'

In contrast, the report gives a sketch of an alternative model of education. Students' sense of power over their own lives can be encouraged by radical curriculum change. The report describes a drama project, involving students from several schools, including Burnage, that centred on the life of a

Manchester boxer and black activist, Len Johnson, 'a story in which racist and sexist conflicts are laid open and bare'. In the course of researching and devising their play, the ideas and values of students changed. They became more critical, more questioning, more self-confident. Using the play and its conflicts as a metaphor for their own lives, 'they were learning about their own culture, the significance of their friendships and relations with each other ... about their attitudes to women and about race and class'.

In many respects, the Burnage Report is a radical counterpoint to the characteristic themes of mainstream rethinking. Like the new realism of a Gould or a Fletcher, it relates to issues at the heart of reform's difficulties and the right's exploitation of them. Although the report's focus rarely strays from events in Manchester schools, there is always a strong sense in which they are treated as a paradigm of wider themes: indeed the report's 'plot', which concerns the inability of both old and new models of education to address central issues of school failure could be read as an allegory of the experience of comprehensive reform. The particular difficulties of a top-down strategy of anti-racism at Burnage can thus come to symbolize more general weaknesses in the programme of reform and the way in which it has been carried out. Insistently, the report returns to the lack of popular involvement at the heart of particular anti-racist strategies, and at the resulting alienation of potential sectors of support. Likewise, it repeatedly draws attention to the contrast between the progressive intentions of anti-racist educators, and the failure of their programme to provide major gains for disadvantaged students, either in terms of education, or of their basic physical security.

To some extent, then, Burnage is retelling some of the story with which the new realism is also concerned. The interpretative tools it employs, however, as well as the conclusions it comes to, are very different. 'Class' and 'democracy' are not used here as they are in Fletcher's articles, and the recommendations of the report have little in common with the outcome of new realist analysis.

Class, for instance, features as much more than an index of deprivation. First, it operates to signify the complexity of students' experience: they do not live their lives simply, or even, in some cases, primarily, as 'Bangladeshi', or 'Irish' or 'English'. Always, the whole way of life upon which the report continually places its stress, involves an ethnic dimension – but also much more than that. Human relations in the school are patterned by other factors too, among which a common social class is central. Following from this insistence upon complexity is the suggestion that the common elements in students' experience offer the possibility of creating an education that stresses, if not a unity, then at least a comparability of experience. It is the school's job to enable students to investigate their experience and what has structured it – in Sartre's phrase, to make sense of the sense history has made of them. In doing so, students, as in the Len Johnson play, would work to pick out the common threads in their experience, and the conflicts that arise around differences of ethnicity and gender.

Haunting these reflections on educational issues is a wider political concern that, like so much of the deep structure of the report, centres on developing a strategy that can address the issues at the heart of the right's appeal without the silences and concessions of the new realism. So, whereas a mainstream response might approach the white backlash that is stimulated by the affirmation of black identities by seeking to play down the anti-racist project, Burnage tries to deal with political hostility by suggesting that the work of positively revaluing a culture and an experience be extended beyond ethnic minorities to the white working class itself. The response to the right would thus take not a moderated, but a more radical form. It is from this perspective that the report attempts to understand how, amid the crises of deindustrialization and the wholesale restructuring of working-class employment and social life, the symbols of white ethnicity can, for a section of white working-class people, conjure up a potent sense of identity. The job of the school is not to retreat in fear before this spectre, but to attempt to provide other ways of interpreting experience and defining identity – a task for which the Len Johnson play stands, albeit sketchily, as a model.

So far, the argument might suggest a familiar and inadequate slogan: 'black and white, unite and fight', with its implication that in the common crucible of economic exploitation, the ethnic differences between the different components of the working class can be melted down. In fact, the report is saying nothing so simple. The differences in experience and perspective between ethnic groups cannot be shelved through a common participation in workplace struggle. Nor – more importantly here – can 'official' anti-racism prevent ethnic conflict. The whole experience of Burnage High School is adduced to demonstrate that top-down anti-racism is more likely to incite resistance than to develop general support. Effective anti-racism can only come about as a result of popular involvement and debate: the dealing with differences by open discussion, the investigation of common experiences, and collective activity. That is why the report places such emphasis upon democratizing life within the school, by recognizing school student organizations. It is why it stresses, too, the need to set up a forum to discuss the school's curriculum with the communities it serves. These bodies would reach out beyond school managements and hand-picked members of ethnic minority groups, to involve students, teachers, and parents from across the whole range of the community in structures where differences could be acknowledged and negotiated, in the context of a commitment to anti-racism and to combating the inequalities that arise around class and gender. None of this implies downplaying the fight of ethnic minority communities against racism, nor the fact of the permeation of white working-class culture by all sorts of racist phenomena. It does, though, entail a belief that an educational politics that can deal effectively with racism, and with other forms of oppression and inequality, must have democracy as its lifeblood. It is with this 'lesson of Burnage' in mind that this book moves on to its final chapter, which will consider the principles of an educational policy that *could* serve as an alternative to that of the right.

6

A different challenge

Last chapters in books of this sort usually convey less the sense of an ending, than the outlining of a 'way forward', a response, an alternative. Not to do so is to have accomplished a critique without hope, or one which relies on the ultimate judgements of Morality or History to condemn forces which in fact require a more immediate demolition. But, in the face of the right's energy and confidence, and the doubts and adaptations of the left, what alternatives are there? Won't a chapter such as this swing towards one of two kinds of temptation? Either to embrace the least evil of the several options in the victors' programme, or to vault over the present time, and proclaim *what might be* if only, through some unforeseeable circumstance, the here and now could be dissolved, and the just city established. Accommodation or Utopianism; the 'real world' of concessions and 'practical politics' or some vision of change that has lost sight of the social forces that might sustain it. Two kinds of desperation, each with their appeal, between which this chapter aims to navigate.

Running within this chapter are clusters of themes which, precisely because of the dangers I have indicated, I do not wish to keep entirely separate. The first is a concern to identify the potential agencies of progressive change, and to suggest the ways in which they must change themselves, if they are to be more than a disapproving chorus or a half-reluctant accomplice of the planned transformations. The second is a treatment of the different levels at which these agencies must work: the immediate campaigns of opposition; the efforts to develop a programme to inspire support for short-term alternatives, that can also point forward to larger possibilities; the creation of a different educational language, in which new aspirations, criticisms and objectives can be discussed; the setting up of exemplary, if small-scale, practical alternatives to dominant

163

curriculum thinking; and the discussion of what a different kind of school system, in a different type of society, could do. In practice, these levels overlap. As the right realizes, apparently local issues can become generally significant, if the political language exists to relate them to wider themes. Likewise, present initiatives can be more easily devised, if there have been elaborated the outlines of an alternative system and its purposes. By connecting agency and purpose, discourse and action, long-term goals and immediate strategies I hope to avoid the polarities that can afflict attempts to work out strategies of opposition.

To begin with the strategies that reformers are now developing for the world after Baker – and with their shortcomings. With the exception of the 'Save ILEA Campaign', the events surrounding the passage of the Education Reform Bill through Parliament were notable for the extraordinary lack of anything that resembled mass campaigning activity. Nor was there a sense in which opponents were keeping their powder dry until the Bill, having become law, presented too close a target to miss. So far as a next phase of opposition to the new policies was concerned, the Labour Party, teacher unions, and most parents' organizations were unprepared.

Yet in other ways a strategy is taking shape, whose premise is the impossibility of complete opposition, even at the level of ideology. It begins by distinguishing two strands in the legislation. Opting out and blanket testing form the first, and are attributed to Mrs Thatcher and the right. The second comprises the national curriculum and local financial management, and reflects the influence of Kenneth Baker. The former tendency is doctrinaire, the latter searches after consensus. The defeated exponents of reform should try to retain influence by supporting the one against the other. There follows from this – not only in the Labour Party but much more widely – the habit of judging the reports of the various committees Baker has set up to provide the detail of the national curriculum less according to principled criteria, than on the degree to which they support the supposed 'Baker' view against full-blooded rightism. The Black Report was thus largely welcomed, even though it is constructed around an idea – national testing – that was for years anathema on the left. The Kingman Report, because it rejected the formal teaching of 'grammar', was likewise seen as a blow against the right, even though it tended to strip English of its cultural and social dimensions. The problem, of course, with this politics of the small mercy is that, having once lost the big battles, it adapts itself to life with the army of occupation. 'The curriculum war is just beginning', argues one educationist. But in reality what is happening on a series of major issues is less a work of resistance than of compliance – subtle, like an old diplomat handling new masters, but nevertheless accepting the framework of change, and planning no great upheavals. The declaration of war, quoted above, continues in terms which suggest the limits of opposition: 'Educational professionals will continue to engage the simplistic nostrums of policy and attempt to convert them into constructive proposals.' The starting point of constructive change remains the 'simplistic nostrums' of government policy – and they cannot be left too far behind

So far, then, we have a history of recent tactics and a strategy for future work which do not give cause for hope that fundamental opposition to the new system is intended. On the evidence of the previous chapter, the same is true of the discourses that surround political action, and of the objectives of policy. Where, then, to start?

Starting Points

The issue of funding has been central to popular struggles in education, and will remain so. The entire education system suffers from chronic under-investment, whose effects on resources and equipment have been documented by successive reports of the Inspectorate, and by the teachers' unions. On top of this general problem, there is the specific crisis of funding in the inner-cities: where need is greatest, recent cuts have been most severe. In its policies for the funding and control of inner-city education, the government is now fairly openly abandoning the majority of students to a system which, already under enormous stress, faces real dangers of a collapse in staffing, morale and student commitment. At the same time, it is planning a selective escape route from this system, through opted-out schools and City Technology Colleges. The contrast between semi-private privilege and widespread misery will be as

165

stark as it ever was.

The tasks of opposition begin here. Built into the Conservative programme is the expectation that parents and schools will use their new-found autonomy to respond to the financial climate with ever more intense efforts at money-saving, fund-raising, and inter-school competition. But there is no reason to assume, a priori, that reflexes of this kind are inevitable. Parents may well act not so much as directors or shareholders in a new educational company, than as political beings who wish to change the logic of the system in which they are operating. The Tories, by increasing the total number of parent-governors to more than 100,000, have created a new layer in civil society which has a distinct and active educational interest. Only the most myopic enthusiasts for 'parent power' can believe that this constituency will, by being placed in a quasi-market situation, automatically start operating as agents of that system. It is possible, at least, that given the right political conditions, some parents will use their new-found access to information, and the authority of their new positions, to start making demands for greater resources. If this were to occur, then the whole new edifice of parental involvement would become unstable. It is for the best organized sections of the reform movement – the NUT, some parents' organizations, the Labour Party – to ensure that this is the direction that most responses take.

The strongest refusal of the logic of the new system is likely to come from the cities. Frequently, it is the tensions and deprivations of the urban experience of education that are stressed, and the fragmentation of the various forces of reform. Teachers confront Labour employers; black communities are impatient of both, and a 'white backlash' is often a latent threat. These divisions can be acute, but they are not the whole story. At several points, the actions of the relatively well-organized teacher unions of the inner-city, where the NUT is in the majority, have made contact with parent and school student opposition to teacher cuts or school closures. Ethnic minority demands have not generally taken the form of 'opting out' of the LEA system, but of demanding improvements within it. Organized teachers have been far from condemning the turbulent discontent of Toxteth and Brixton, Tottenham and

Birmingham: the reaction of NUT branches in these areas has been to criticize racism, poverty and policing, and to recognize the energies and thwarted aspirations of black communities. These various points of contact have not, of course, been constant, and now, more than ever, the relations between the different elements in inner-city education politics are under strain. When teachers strike against job loss, the effects are felt first by students, who sense, after a time, a loss of educational opportunity, and by parents, who are given a sudden new burden of child care. There is a limit to how often this can happen before their support for protest against cuts is called into question. There are other strains too. Every time a Labour council, like Kirklees in the case of Dewsbury, backs away from anti-racism, pressures from ethnic minorities for opting out will grow. Conversely, for every bungled programme of anti-racist education, there will be new converts to the ideas of the right. Nevertheless, the urban experience of campaigning is a rich one, that includes both militant action and Burnage-like demands for greater democracy and changes in the curriculum.

Politically, within the urban educational experience, the resources exist to make of the government's programme for the inner-city a national scandal that is symbolic of the whole direction of Conservative policy. In the same way as the word 'Brent' came to stand for the right's entire critique of local authority reform, so the condition of schooling in London or Liverpool can become an indictment of 'two nations' politics. The controlling Labour Parties, the teachers' unions and community organizations between them are capable of mobilising thousands of people in militant forms of protest. Just as the right has relied on anecdote and dramatic incident to take its points, so too can its opponents; there are many ways of dramatizing cuts and shortages. Recurring and co-ordinated protest forms the best context for the presentation of alternative ideas on funding, and on education generally. For this to take place, however, requires an enormous investment of collective and undivided energy. The question is: can it happen?

The counter-pressures are strong. Although there is a history of recent popular struggle for resources, there exist also all the problems of yesterday's defeats and the new realist response to them. It is difficult to see the analysis supported by Neil

Fletcher, for instance, culminating in the unity of teachers and Labour Party against government policy. And if militant trade union action is an insufficient strategy with which to mobilize a widespread opposition, still less realistic are those which forswear any degree of militancy in favour of appeals to a public opinion that is often nebulously invoked, but rarely sought out in its more active, campaigning forms. The most effective policy will be one which is based from the beginning on a combined strategy of 'industrial' and 'community' action. Many of the elements that could combine in such a strategy do not need to be invented. They exist in the recent past: in the way teachers have used selective strike action to free their members for public campaigning, in parents' petitions and self-organized referenda, in community campaigns on the level and character of provision, in school students' picketing of County Hall to protest against teacher job loss. The problem is one of creating from these diverse activities a strategy that does not decline into syndicalist protest or become a mere ancillary activity to a council's role in managing scarce resources, but which is capable rather of sustaining a unity of opposition to government policy. The strategy has to be negotiated: that is to say, it should not be the result of unilateral decisions by teachers, or by parent groups. Because it would be negotiated, it would be a compromise – but a compromise between allies. In the first instance, it would be a compromise on tactical questions of how to mobilize against government policy. It would need to take into account the value of 'industrial action' as a major impetus to campaigning, as well as the necessity of finding forms of action that maximized parents' support. It would need to ensure that the platform of any campaign was not limited to the demands of any one sector, but that it was broad enough to include both issues that relate to the interests of those who worked in education, and the concerns of those who are served by it. In taking this last step, towards a 'political' platform, it would leave the area of defensive campaigns against cuts, to set out what would inevitably be an alternative education policy. Later in this chapter, I will try to set out some possible elements of such a policy. For now it is enough to stress how it would be most effective if it arose – like that of the right – from the experience of particular campaigns.

Developing alternatives

For some readers, what is written above will seem no more than agitprop, that can lay no claim to the high ground of educational argument, and constitutes no convincing alternative to the programme of the right. I prefer to see it as the setting out of conditions necessary to the fuller development of such an alternative, in the same way as the offensives of the new right and the defeat of teacher militancy were necessary for the introduction of the Education Reform Act. Necessary but not – of course – sufficient: opposition to cuts, however lively and well-supported, cannot in itself revitalize the programme of reform. Its traditional policies have run into the sand. Caught between the demands of industry and the needs of the individual, damaged by criticism from within, and their insufficiencies revealed by the cultural polemic of the right, they are simply not able to generate answers to the problems and failures of contemporary education. Access and resources remain central to any programme of the left, but unless it also relates to questions of educational democracy and the content of the curriculum, it will be defeated by its opponents. The ERA starkly demonstrates the major form defeat will take – but it is not the only one. Just as likely, on present evidence, is the incorporation of diluted themes of the right within the reforming programme. Sincere and self-destructive homage of this sort is already being paid, in Neil Fletcher's belief that when he brandishes terms like 'standards' and 'choice' he is recalling the era of the 'socialist educational prophets'. This ransacking of the right's intellectual baggage in search of the lost commandments of socialism will achieve no results beneficial to Labour's constituency, and will only increase the extent of disillusion; no programme to raise standards will be successful unless it rethinks its attitude to the knowledge and experience of the students it is addressing, and the motives and purposes which it assigns to learning.

Such efforts, though, cannot be the work solely of educational professionals – and it is here that the idea of a negotiated programme takes on a second level of importance. One reason for the unharassed ease with which the right has played upon the divergence between producer and consumer interests has been a tradition of curricular and pedagogic reform that owes far too much to ideas generated among teachers, and too little to informed popular debate. The vast new structures of parental involvement and control are built around this argument: it is time, said the right, that parents exercised control over these ingrained professional habits of experimenting on their young. Teachers' first, unsurprising reaction to the new institutions of parent power was defensive. Aware of the origins of the new Annual Parents' Meeting and of the ways in which its structures permit discussion of the work of individual staff, the NUT advised its members that, if invited, they should not attend. Teachers generally noted with satisfaction the low attendance at the meetings. Such reactions were mistaken. Far from recoiling into a professional defensiveness which can only further encourage their opponents, teachers, with their allies among parents, should be trying to breathe some life into the rather inert structures of parental involvement. But, to put it plainly, when they turn up at these meetings, what do they say? And when in other contexts they might discuss alternative educational programmes, where could they look for ideas? Not – I hope – to some modified version of the rhetoric of modernization. Nor to the recycled truisms of the 'equal opportunity' years. I have already tried to indicate that Conservative modernization is neglectful or destructive of many areas of human need. Experience has shown, more powerfully than I can, the weaknesses of the reforming tradition. Yet satisfying answers of other sorts are not available. So to construct a programme that tries from a radical and democratic point of view to respond to the issues raised in commonplace discussion about education – about school and work, the rights of parents and students, raising standards, and what education should be for – entails journeying through experiences and arguments that, though they do not always arise from reflections about schooling, nevertheless centre on the purposes of learning and its relevance to those who do not enjoy wealth or power. Such a journey would not be a kind of expedition in search of panaceas. It would rather be a process of studying particular ideas and ways of working to see if there was anything in their method or conclusions that, modified to suit this time and place, could be of use.

Modern, democratic, intellectual

These intellectual excursions can best begin with a return to the heyday of progressive ideas, before those processes began that assimilated them to a mass education system anything but radical in its intent. When progressivism first took its distinctive twentieth-century shape, it aligned itself, like other modernist movements, with the left. Particularly in the work of the American John Dewey – though not so much in England, where older, romantic influences held sway – it synthesized a critique of archaic authoritarianism with an attraction towards the new, urban experience, in which 'stimuli of an intellectual sort pour in upon us in all kinds of ways', and with a political commitment to 'a state of affairs in which the interest of each in his work is uncoerced and intelligent'. Dewey welcomed all these signs of the new, and sought an education that moved with the grain of the times. He was confident that large-scale industry and urbanization were rendering useless those residues of aristocratic education which still existed in parts of the school system. Present-day industry had created the conditions for a 'common, democratic life', even if the 'desire for private profit' inhibited the realization of this promise. The school, renovating itself, could become a centre for enabling the rebirth of democracy, while at the same time it prepared its students for productive life. For this brief moment, progressivism occupied a ground that commanded all areas of educational debate: it linked together modernization, democracy and intellectual development in a vision whose attractiveness is still compelling. From Dewey, as from so many intellectuals of the early twentieth-century modern movement, the reader gathers a sense of the writer's openness to questions of social transformation. The industrialization and cultural change experienced by the capitalisms of Europe and America form the matrix but not the limits of his thought: he is prepared to envisage further change to unlock the potentialities that are present in the new social systems, but which will not be released so long as political control remains in a few hands.

In the time of reform, when progressive education achieved important influence, it retained many of the terms of democratic modernization but in a form whose rhetorical nature became clearer as time passed. With the progressivism of the reforming years, proclamations of the harmony of individual development and economic need served not as a description of how things might be, but of how they actually were at the present time. In the local version of this process, 'democracy' became a term to describe the modern British society and state. The language shifted from the near-visionary to the apologetic. The effect, nevertheless, was to block the conversion of education into an instrument for responding directly to those ideas of economic need that are now embodied in vocationalism. So long as it could be claimed that individual development *per se* was a good thing for the economy, then the reformers' equation of individual and societal need could be maintained. But in the education of the 1980s, the unity of 'democracy, intellect and modernization' was most blatantly scattered: democracy has become another term for 'choice'; modernization is squarely based on employer need; ideas about the development of the individual have become mixed up with justifications for inequality.

Democracy

The three terms at work in Dewey's system remain central to a programme for challenging present hegemonies. The first of them, democracy, can be elaborated in relation to almost every aspect of the education system. At present, a lack of democracy drains away motivation and commitment from students and from teachers. On the other hand, a particular form of parent democracy, built around increased involvement in school administration, serves to create an commitment that is intense, but limited in its responsibilities, and productive of greater inequalities between schools. The attention devoted to it by the ERA masks the assumption of greater powers by the central state, which has taken from elected local bodies the capability to determine educational needs and make plans to meet them. The task of the opponents of Conservatism is to develop a democratic programme that can appeal to people's desires to exercise responsibility for learning and for what happens in their lives. Unlike the versions of the right, however, this alternative would aim to extend democratic practice into areas of education where at present authoritarian rule prevails. It would also seek to give a deeper and more radical meaning to the term 'democracy', pulling it away from the orbit of individual choice towards one of collective determination of policies that recognized the needs of all. For students, particularly beyond primary level, this would mean having a genuine say in what happens to them at school. As a basic working rule, they should have the right not to determine, but to negotiate, their curriculum. They would be encouraged to use the school as a resource to throw light on the issues that affected their lives, within a guiding framework established by the school, which would seek to ensure that they had a broad and balanced education. Beyond the curriculum, as the Burnage Inquiry suggests, there should exist the right to form independent school student bodies. As Hugh Lauder has explained, the purposes of this general introduction of democracy into student life would be to raise achievement through increasing personal autonomy, and to transform the attitudes of students and of teachers, so that their relationship was based less on a mutually suspicious accommodation, and more on the joint pursuit of an empowering kind of learning.

Democracy would not stop with student life. One precondition for the involvement of teachers in efforts to remodel learning is the lifting of what has in effect been the persecution of their unions. Another is the recognition that effective curriculum development will not take place without teachers' active and committed consent. This implies a reversal of the trend towards greater managerial authority in the schools. But greater democracy within the school would mean little without a change in the relationship between the school and the world outside it. Present laws restrict 'community' influence on the school to LEA representatives (fewer in number than they used to be), the police, representatives of business, committees to determine matters of religious education, and parents. In some cases, LEAs have been able to apply these regulations creatively, to interpret, for instance, 'business' representation to include trade unionists. Nevertheless, linked to a system of parental choice, the law reinforces a form of decision-making which combines authoritarian direction with the influence of a market. It is necessary to link the school to different influences. Parental involvement in the work of the school and in decision-making can be increased without policies of open enrolment and opting out. Different structures should be found – again, perhaps, of the sort that Burnage suggested – that allow general involvement, especially by disadvantaged groups, in debate about school policy, including curriculum policy, and purpose. Governing bodies are both too restricted in their brief and too unrepresentative of oppressed groups to allow this.

This point brings the argument to a problem that Dewey's generation did not approach. Formal procedures of democracy are inadequate if they do not advance the interests of disadvantaged groups: in some areas, for instance, the 1988 procedures for the election of greater numbers of parent governors actually seem to have resulted in a decrease in elected governors from ethnic minorities. The simple, 'colour-blind' application of the first-past-the-post system works to exclude whole groups of people. Since similar processes of exclusion work throughout education, a programme of democracy entails deliberately increasing the weight of those groups who are usually on its margins: women, ethnic minorities, working-class people in general. There need to be measures which increase resources and target them at particular groups; which improve these groups' access to education – especially at higher levels – which increase their representation on governing bodies and in some cases among the teaching force; and which swing the focus of the curriculum round towards a content relevant to their experience and empowering of their aspirations.

Access, resources, the curriculum, the work of teachers and systems of control are all involved in a programme for democracy. An undemocratic programme of modernization may benefit some but will not achieve its proclaimed objectives. It is impossible to imagine a sharp general rise in educational achievement without policies of this kind: the commitment to learn, and to provide the conditions for learning, would not be there. If modernization is understood as a policy of equipping all students with skills and understandings that improve their life chances, and at the same time are of general social and economic benefit, then democracy is essential to it. But to say this is not yet to touch upon more precise issues of the curriculum, nor to be able to answer in a different way those questions that vocationalism has made its own: how can the school prepare its students for work, and what kind of understanding should it deliver of the economic system upon which the life of the country depends? It is to find satisfactory answers to these questions that we must turn from democracy to another key term in Dewey's perspective.

The modern

The meaning of 'modern' has changed since Dewey used it. Mass-production industry, that grouped people together in ever-larger numbers, and led to the sweeping away of archaic political influences, provided the forms of social life which allowed him to speak of a common experience, and of the possibility of exercising collective control over it. In the versions of 'education and the economy' that are now most influential, mass-production industry is obsolescent; the future belongs to the small-scale producer and the service provider. Common ownership and economic planning have no place in this vision, and organized labour will be weak. Those who thrive will be interested not so much in exercising control over the way the system works, as in adapting themselves, with entrepreneurial enthusiasm, to the demands it makes and the opportunities it offers.

An alternative to the present modernization programme, that recovers something of Dewey's collectivist optimism, would begin from a different economic understanding. It would not agree that, in the core sectors of the economy, mass production has had its day. It would deny that a viable economy can be constructed around finance, the service sector and the British offshoots of multi-national capital. It would reject the idea that the spontaneous order of the market can, especially in the context of the fundamental weaknesses of the British economy, produce a stable economic base. It would see the attempts to organize an education and training system on the cheap not as a solution to these problems, but as a new twist in their accentuation. It would demand an economic strategy that was interventionist to an extent way beyond the indecisive efforts of Conservative modernization.

Thus far, however, there is nothing from which the more far-sighted capitalist planner would dissent. The deeper differences are in the ideas of economic need and purpose that underlie an alternative system. It would not simply restate, in modern terms, the case against an economy subject by its nature to periodic crisis, mass unemployment and waste of resources. It would in addition move off in different directions, which are well summarized by Hilary Wainwright, in a commentary on ten years of 'workers' plans' and local council initiatives. What she says allows an excursion into another area that is rich with implications for an alternative education programme. First would be a concern not just with growth of production, but with the 'nature of commodities and services themselves and their technology, whether they are weapons, pollutants, unsafe deodorants, unhealthy food or unresponsive public services'. Second, would be an emphasis on the 'quality of working conditions', that would include, besides health and safety, questions relating to skilling and deskilling, to control of the labour process and the length of the working day. It would also look at systems of control and status in the workplace, with special emphasis on their race and gender-based qualities.

Carried into education, these ideas would bring several radical kinds of change. The experience-based nature of much current exploration of the work process would be retained, but the issues investigated would be much broader than those of even the most liberal of TVEI schemes. The division of labour in the workplace and the way the workforce is managed would be examined at first hand. The purpose of a particular economic activity and its consequences – ecological and social – for the rest of humanity could also be opened to question. Broad theoretical knowledge of a kind essential to understanding modern society, and to making decisions about its direction, would be linked to detailed questions about the experience of work. The 'Youngian' theory of the division between the practical and the intellectual would be refuted.

Even at present, it should be possible to put into operation some of these principles, by pressing TVEI curricula to their limits and by organizing work experience to serve broadly-defined educational ends. In a not unimaginable future, in which local councils have some of their functions restored to them, the principles could be further developed. The GLC on a small scale tried to support or popularize alternative kinds of productive activity. It had a policy of investment in skills, rather than in deskilling methods of production. It supported projects of technological innovation designed to be socially useful. It sponsored training in authentic skills for sections of the workforce traditionally excluded from access to them. It encouraged co-operatives, worker-user associations, and so on. At the same time, it accompanied these immediately practical initiatives with investigation of the often hidden workings of multi-nationals and international finance and their effects on the economy of London. The combination is an educationally attractive one. It suggests a skill training that is set in a broader educational context and connects the immediate experience of the workplace to much wider relationships. In this area, the broken links of Dewey's original model could be restored, and it would be possible to speak of a modernizing educational project that really was related to intellectual development of diverse kinds, and was inspired by the perfectly democratic aim of empowering people to take control of their working lives. The opposition that such a project would arouse is almost too obvious to need stating: for mass education to claim the right to examine and make judgements on the economic process is unheard of. It invites the obdurate resistance of employers. As a large-scale project, thus, it awaits much more favourable political conditions. As a collection of smaller-scale initiatives, utilizing public sector or small enterprise resources, it can do exemplary work.

So far, what I have written about the curriculum draws from and updates earlier socialist and progressive traditions. Polytechnic education, the educational ideology of the Soviet Union in its first years, had 'the aim of studying modern technology in general, its main achievements and its foundations, the inter-relationship between the various branches of production and developmental tendencies of modern technology'. Knowledge of this kind would be acquired, in the main, by first-hand experience – through investigation of particular work processes, and through working for a time in agriculture or industry. It would not only be intended for vocational purposes, but for the all-round development of the worker: 'Today he carries out orders, tomorrow he can be an inventor, and the day after tomorrow an important organiser in the factory.' Pronouns apart, it is an attractive vision. The breadth of its interest in work, and its stress on learning through experience and activity retain their importance today. In several ways, though, it is too narrow a base for an alternative education. It does not, for instance, address the vast areas of life outside work. People do not acquire understandings about their place in the world, do not develop desires and moral principles, solely from the work process. It is because they don't that the right's cultural agitation has had an impact, and that race is an important feature of educational politics. In its neglect of areas like these, polytechnicism is no more attentive to the experiences, cultures and identities of students than the modernizing education of Britain in the 1980s. Thus, to centre a curriculum on a programme of 'radical vocationalism' is inadequate. It must be complemented by a wider cultural concern, not simply for the sake of an all-round education, but because it is through thinking about cultural relationships that one of the most central and difficult questions of education is posed: how are the school and the student to negotiate the relationship between the culture from which the student comes, and the formal requirements of even the most child-centred of school curricula. It is in responding to this question that alternatives to Conservatism will approach the third aspect of Dewey's triad, that concerns intellectual development. Answering it is vital to issues of student motivation, to achievement and standards, and to the whole vexed question of the purposes of education.

Intellectual development

Broadly, there have been, in debate on the left, three ways of responding to issues that concern the relationship between formal education and working-class students. The first, deriving its authority from Gramsci, emphasizes the result for the intellectual development of members of subordinate classes, of those classes' social position. In Gramsci's writings on language, for instance, the effects of living a hegemonized relationship with the dominant culture are underlined with great force. Gramsci was a Sardinian. He spoke the language fluently and encouraged it as the language of learning for small children. His letters are full of dialect terms, affectionately remembered. But when he considers dialect from a political and an educational perspective, his opinion shifts. Dialect is a relic of the past. It is 'fossilized and anachronistic', utterly inseparable from the consciousness of a subordinate class, and utterly incapable of serving as a medium in which to discuss the workings of the world outside the home, the farm and the market place. It is something to be combatted, in the name of a struggle to 'create a common national language, the non-existence of which creates friction, particularly in the popular masses, among whom local particularisms and phenomena of a narrow and provincial mentality are more tenacious than is believed'. Those present-day writers who endorse this element in Gramsci's thought reiterate his insistence on the qualitative gap that exists between the organized, formal knowledge of the school curriculum, which represents a rational selection from centuries of culture, and the spontaneous and intellectually under-developed understandings of the student. Harold Entwistle's book on Gramsci's educational views, boldly subtitled *Conservative Schooling for Radical Politics*, is the essential statement of this case: the best service that the school can give students from subordinate classes is to take them to the highest standards of the education evolved by classes which have devoted centuries of effort to the creation of authoritative systems of knowledge. Maureen Stone has applied a similar argument to the education of Afro-Caribbean students in English schools: to centre the curriculum on what is immediately relevant to students is to leave them no further forward than when they started their learning. What students and parents want is the best of present-day education and not some patronizing selection of 'relevant' and easily-digestible material.

Other pedagogies, equally firm in their claim to radicalism, have developed opposing ideas. They criticize the official knowledge of the school, stressing its remoteness from the experience of students, and the fact that it is wrapped up in a mystique and an authoritarian pedagogy which are enough in practice to exclude most students from involvement. By contrast, they encourage and celebrate the self-expression of students, through talk, autobiographical writing, narrative and

179

poetry. Their intention is by these means to unlock potentialities which the dominant forms of schooling keep pent up.

Neither approach is without its difficulties. The first leaves out of the account some major difficulties of the learning process: the fraught relationship between spontaneous and organized thought in a system where the organization of knowledge is so entwined with the systems of social domination. The second, empathizing with the oppressed, makes a positive evaluation of the experience of subordinate groups. It does not, however, come to terms with the issues posed by Gramsci: that for a subordinate group to understand its position, and to identify its goals and aspirations is no simple process of affirmation. His stress on the way that the experiences of most individuals have been most deeply affected by the hegemony of stronger groups is an antidote to facile suggestions that the self-affirmation of the oppressed, in the form of 'finding a voice' can itself strengthen understanding of wider social relations, and enable action to change them.

There is a third approach. From a number of different disciplines – history, sociology, literature – and several points of origin – sociologists of autobiography in France, radical educationists in Australia and the United States, the historian Carlo Ginzburg in Italy – there is developing a concern to explore the meeting grounds of spontaneous experience and systematized knowledge, and, in the same process, the connections between subjectivity and wider historical process. Both kinds of relationship are suggested in Gramsci's famously allusive comment: 'The starting point of critical elaboration is the consciousness of what one really is, and is knowing thyself as a product of the historical process to date, which has deposited in you an infinity of traces, without leaving an inventory.' The starting point here is experience, but it is an experience understood as historically-structured and not immediately accessible to consciousness. The remark suggests that through a kind of historically-based self-analysis, it is possible to understand a multitude of historical and social tendencies.

Gramsci, then, sees in the culture of subordinate groups the material for a complex work of investigation, that will have to seek out the slightest influences upon the individual, from the most scanty evidence. At other points in his writing, he extends this stress on complexity to the system of popular knowledge: it is, he says, a combination of received and more or less mystifying ideas, and 'good sense', that expresses a practical attitude to the world, and is open to suggestions that it should be changed. In both respects – the complexity of the culture and of the knowledge systems within it – Gramsci outlines an attitude very different from that which has usually dominated educational debate. David Hargreaves, for instance, can find no place in the curriculum for 'working-class culture', save that which is concerned with the most immediate problems of everyday life. And, like the commissioners who interviewed children in the last century, and concluded from their ignorance about royalty, the apostles and other important figures, that they possessed little that counted as knowledge, teachers still now grossly under-rate the knowledge and experience that students bring to the school. Students are, after all, curious and actively knowledgeable about the world, and popular knowledge is a 'wide and subtle' field. The problem is, as Daniel Bertaux writes, that 'each person has but a limited field of perception. Even if people are quite conscious of the local rules of the game in the part of society that surrounds them, they usually have no way to accede to a knowledge of the whole, much less to an understanding of the historical movement of the whole.' The model of education suggested by Gramsci's remarks asks students to move towards an understanding of this whole by commencing with an examination of personal experience, so as to identify in it those signs of the working of larger processes. From the simplest of questions – why do I want to become a nursery nurse? Why did my parents come to this country? Why do I smile to myself when a teacher tells me off? – a wider world of socialization and resistance, history and political economy is opened up. From personal experience, understanding can – suitably taught, for explorations of this sort are not spontaneous – arch out critically into wider surveys.

In the course of such investigation, not only are hidden areas of experience opened up, but those ideologies and habits of thought that kept them hidden are also thrown into question. Thus education of this sort as much concerns the 'tools of thought' as it does the raw material of inquiry. Trevor Pateman lists the processes that are active in present-day culture and inhibit the development of learning: the idea that knowledge breeds insecurity, and that certain kinds of knowledge – of social powerlessness, for instance – are best not confronted; decisions that other satisfactions are more easily available; the idea that since nothing can be changed, non-instrumental learning is pointless; the social taboos that surround certain areas of discussion and investigation, from sexuality to politics. To these restrictions on knowledge, and on the impulse to know, should be added others, that stem less from feelings of resignation and powerlessness on the part of subordinate social groups, than from the direct effects of the dominance of a particular class: the 'amnesiac rendering of the past' prevalent in modern culture; the lack of availability of interpretative schemes that would allow people to make sense of their own experience, and of the changes in their lives. These are powerful disincentives to learning, that the school either perpetuates or does not sufficiently oppose. Except for the trivialization of social relations now found in subjects like 'personal and social education', the school's version of knowledge exists in a form too often sealed off from the experiences and problems of students' lives. Approaching a knowledge so remote, students feel that ideas and complexities and abstractions are somehow weapons used against them to keep them out of an area labelled 'learning', and not tools for their own use.

The alternative is not, in a fake gesture of radicalism, to dismiss 'abstraction' as an instrument of the dominators. It is to insist that abstractions are approached through the experience of students, and that they are used to illuminate the issues of students' own lives. 'How do you get somebody to understand an abstraction?' asks Judith Williamson. 'By relating it to the reality that it is an abstraction of.' But since schools do not in the first place address much of this reality, intellectual development is stunted. 'Without an intimate and complex relationship', writes Williamson, echoing Vygotsky, 'between their own experience and the conceptual plane which allows the possibility of representing and changing experience, all they learn is the concepts and principles as a pattern or system, complete in itself.' The result is intellectual nervousness, apathy, resistance. But in the process of the difficult encounters between organized and spontaneous knowledge, it is possible to imagine students' own wishes and drives being tapped to provide the momentum of learning, rather than resisting it. Students will then have discovered some real need – a desire to understand one's self in a particular way, or to explore some alternative way of dealing with the possibilities that are open to them in their lives – which education will have served.

A negotiated challenge

These excursions, I hope, have not been detours. They have not left the highway of policy-centred campaigning only in order to ramble among the forests of the left's memory and imagination. The questions they have explored seem to me, as I think they seemed to Dewey, important to the formation of an intellectually commanding programme, and to the creation of a new 'language' in which educational content and purpose can be discussed. On the basis of their treatment of issues relating to achievement and motivation, curriculum content and educational control, I shall now return and try to answer the question which was posed in the early part of the chapter: what would a programme look like, that intended to rally support for simple principles which could demonstrate alternatives to Conservative policy, while also pointing forward to larger possibilities?

To repeat another earlier point: such a programme has to be negotiated. Literally, if the real forces assembled who could take it up. Figuratively, in that it has to take account of the educational landscape as Conservatism has shaped it, and not how progressives, reformers or leftists would like it to be. Thus, it has to be concerned with defence of existing educational provision. It has to set out some basic organizational and curriculum principles that are opposed to those of the right, without falling Jack Straw-like into the arms of the modernizing tendency. It has to put forward a democratic basis for a popular education.

It thus has the task, not only of being a post-Conservative document, but also a rethinking of the programme of reform. What follows is a first effort, to develop the excursions of the previous pages, into one part of an educational strategy – defensive on many issues, bolder on others – that suits our hard times.

A Charter for schools

Preamble

The government is creating an economy and a political system based on the principle of two nations. It thrives on the promotion of inequality. Benefits flow to the rich. Banking and finance boom, while in many areas deindustrialization continues apace. Trade unions are attacked, and the welfare state undermined. But as well as rewarding the privileged and crushing the oppressed, Tory policy has another aim: to create among the middle sectors of society a set of 'client groups' which will see economic or political advantage in the effects of Thatcherism. Tory policies on housing, and on share-ownership are geared to this purpose. Education is now the next in line: another area where the Tories employ the powers of the central state to break up established interests, and create the conditions in which some sections of the population – not only the richest – will be given access to greater privilege, while others will experience the bitter effects of Tory inequality.

No aspect of education has escaped the grip of Conservative policy. The government is creating a system which will combine the worst features of central control with the inequalities of a market system. Selection will be increased; disparities of status, quality and resources between schools will grow; segregation and discrimination by race will be tolerated, if not encouraged. A national curriculum, monitored by blanket testing, will transmit Conservative values throughout the system, and the call for schools to serve the needs of 'industry' will continue to place an uncritical treatment of issues of work and the economy at the heart of secondary schooling. The public schools, their populations swollen over recent years, will continue to enjoy their privileges.

To service the new system, Conservatives want a different kind of teaching force. What they teach will be subject to central control. Their unions are under attack; national negotiating rights have been eradicated; headteachers and education

184

authorities have been given the opportunity and the power to define teachers' conditions of service in new and more rigorous ways. Systems of managerial assessment of teachers will soon be in in force. In short, teachers will be the tightly-disciplined agents of delivery of the Conservative curriculum.

Cuts and privatization threaten the jobs of many others in the schools. The workers, mainly women, who clean the schools, or who serve the dinners, face either the loss of their jobs, or cuts in wages, as councils are forced by law to put their services out to tender.

Parents will have no say in what is taught: the national curriculum will take it out of their hands. Their influence will be that of 'consumers' of education, who compete against each other for their children's entry to the most highly-favoured schools. Under a system of open enrolment, and 'local financial management' of schools, it will be the effects of parent choice, not of planning, that determine whether schools thrive or close, and how well-resourced they are. Governing bodies, with a larger parent representation, will become 'boards of directors' of schools that will have to use every available advantage or means of marketing to attract the students who can ensure their survival. For every parent who seizes the opportunity of 'choice', there will be many others whose children suffer the effects of an unplanned and unequal system.

Students face new denials of their rights and their experiences. Compulsory YTS schemes cut the youth wage, lower expectations and discipline the attitudes of school-leavers. Types of education which relate to the special experiences of girls, of black students, of lesbians and gays are firmly, even vehemently, discouraged. Patterns of unequal opportunity are reinforced.

All this amounts to a sustained and fundamental attack on the policies of equal opportunity which developed in the thirty-five years following the Education Act of 1944. Yet the response which it has met is strangely muted. Educationists, Labour and trade union leaders have either themselves joined in the criticisms of the old system, or else have suggested that the best that can be done is to mitigate the worst effects of Tory policy, by supporting its milder forms against the excesses of the right.

We reject both approaches. There was much that was wrong

185

with post-war education: whatever the intentions of teachers, it was inadequate in its responses to inequality; it neglected or found little value in the experiences of black or working-class students, and the communities they came from. It reproduced sexist ideas and divisions. Too often, it mimicked the curriculum and values of selective, or even of private, education. Too often, it offered its students little understanding of the social processes which were shaping their lives.... Yet it was developing. It did raise, though insufficiently, students' levels of understanding and achievement. The framework of equal opportunity offered a home to genuinely progressive efforts to develop a relevant education. No useful purpose is served by attacking it on grounds that give comfort to the right.

Conversely, it is wrong to think that the few useful developments in the education of the 1980s are grounds for welcoming a general, Conservative-led 'revolution in education and training'. In some parts of the curriculum – several TVEI schemes stand out – teachers have taken advantage of the 'space' opened up by new, well-funded projects, to initiate activity-based, collaborative, problem-solving work. But this hasn't altered the drive of the Tory system towards greater selectiveness, nor the fact that these progressive changes in work-orientated education are accompanied by the promotion of values that raise little criticism of the established economic order.

An alternative strategy to that of the Tories can't rely only upon mitigating their worst effects, or on taking advantage of whatever 'progressive' opportunities remain. It has to address a full range of issues.

It is to suggesting the basis of such an alternative that we now turn our attention.

Defence

The most favourable context for developing support for socialist education policies is action in defence of the real and immediate concerns of parents, teachers, school students and the community. These concerns include the following:
- To resist the effects of cuts in spending, ranging from lack of books to worsening pupil-teacher ratios, to school closures.

186

- To defend the school meals, cleaning and caretaking services against cuts in wages, provisions, conditions and jobs.
- To defend equal opportunities policies and practices against Tory attacks on them, and from retreats by LEA's.
- To defend unstreamed teaching against pressure to increase streaming, at primary as well as secondary levels.
- To defend a broad curriculum, not dictated by vocationalism, by narrow and rigid forms of assessment, or by Tory values of nation and 'family'.
- To defend teachers victimised because they do not conform to these new models of education – e.g. as a result of Section 28 of the Local Government Act, or of the clauses in the 1986 Education Act concerning 'political education'.
- To campaign against any school preparing to opt out.
- To minimize the negative effects of open enrolment, by calling for, among other things, extra resources for schools facing falls in roll as a result of that policy.

The aims of education

We believe that the existing political and economic arrange-ments of society are such as to reinforce inequalities, to stifle creative potential, and to develop the personality in competitive ways. We believe that the school, even after much reforming effort, still reflects this wider system. Access to advanced education is still disproportionately denied to girls, and to black and working-class students. The content, and the hidden curriculum, of education leaves the majority of students with a deep sense of the unimportance of their own lives and with no conviction that knowledge can, in any broad, social, non-vocational sense, be really useful.

We believe that education, in and out of school, should concern:
- The development of people's creative potential.
- The development of students' understanding of the natural world, of the society in which they live, and of the work processes of that society.

187

- The development of the capacity to work with others in controlling society's collective life.

Organization

We stand for a social programme which guarantees employment and standards of housing, welfare and health provision that would lay the foundation for meaningful access to education. We call for support for a wide-ranging programme of measures to oppose inequalities, to raise the level of achievement of students, and to create an education that can promote the confidence and understanding to participate in the democratic control of society. These measures should include:

- Resourcing the school system so as to increase the educational opportunities available to working-class students: nursery education for all whose parents want it; greatly reduced class size; staffing levels adequate to provide a wide range of teaching strategies, with support for special needs, English as a Second Language, curriculum development and implementation; an expansion of post-16 education, with a system of allowances for all those staying on.
- Transforming the system of public examinations, so that they no longer serve as 'cut-off' points which restrict access to employment and further education. At any time in their post-14 educational career, students should be able to accumulate credits for particular courses, which would build up to certificated qualifications.
- Creating a single unified system of fully comprehensive schools under local democratic control, without private, voluntary or selective enclaves.
- Integrating the education of adults and school students. All workers should have the right to educational sabbaticals, and schools, like other educational institutions, should have the resources to provide for them.

Curriculum

Organizational change is not enough. There must also be changes to the curriculum to make it relevant to the experience

188

of the majority of school students, capable of giving an accurate picture of social reality, and of engaging their interest:

- Wherever appropriate, learning should be activity-based, and organized around student inquiry. The community should be used as an educational resource, and as material for critical investigation.
- The curriculum should encompass areas of knowledge such as philosophy, psychology, economics, sociology, that are essential to understanding modern society, and that the Tories will not tolerate, or will accept only in diluted form.
- The curriculum should be attentive to the real cultures of the people who live in Britain. It should not transmit the versions of the national culture promoted by the dominant class in society. The culture which students bring to the school with them – including community languages – should be neither disregarded nor patronized, but should be at the centre of many aspects of the curriculum. At the same time, schools should aim to develop in all students the conceptual and linguistic advantages that the dominant group has long enjoyed.
- Schools should consciously organize to develop an internationalist, not an anglocentric, curriculum, and to discourage the racism, sexism and heterosexism which affect the lives of many students.
- All students should study science and technology, both in their technical aspects, and in terms of their social and ecological effects. Likewise, both the techniques employed in the world of work, and the social relations and social consequences of work should be studied.

We think that such a programme would raise the levels of achievement of the majority of the school population, and create the basis for a different attitude to learning. Whereas its basic outline would be the outcome of a national process of decision-making, every encouragement would be given to local initiatives to devise curricula and teaching methods that take up the general themes. We need more experimentation, not less.

189

Democracy

Schools should be centres of initiative, responsive to the communities in which they are placed. Democracy should be fundamental to their ethos and their functioning. We call for measures to increase democracy and collective participation in the work of the school and in the planning of education policy. We call for:

- Democracy among teaching staff, with curriculum and associated decisions made through collective discussion not management dictation.
- Meetings of all who work in a school to discuss matters of common interest and to break down professional barriers.
- Measures to increase the openness of schools to parents, including an open access policy.
- The promotion of trade unionism, through opposition to privatization, the restoration of teachers' negotiating rights, and the establishment of agreements that safeguard conditions of service.
- Secondary students would have the right to organize and to be consulted, and would be represented on a school's governing body.
- Local democratic control of schools. Decisions about educational planning, resources and the broad framework of curriculum policy would be taken by education authorities which had been broadened to include representatives of community groups, parents, trade unions, and so on. School governing bodies, which should comprise LEA, parent, teacher and student representatives, should oversee the implementation of this policy at school level.
- An end to the educational role of the undemocratic and unaccountable MSC. Transfer of its functions to elected local authorities.

It is difficult, of course, to contain in the form of a manifesto, the range of issues which have made the educational debates of the last ten years so thematically dense. The charter, however, makes some attempt to do so. It tries to combine the elaboration of what could be called ideological themes, with directly political demands. Everything I have written in this last chapter argues for such a combination, that is essential to matching and surpassing the Conservative achievement. The right turn, since its beginnings in the late sixties, has become sharper with every year of my working life. I have spent this time as a kind of involuntary participant observer, trying to understand and to respond to the policy of the right, and its impact on the lives of those connected with school education. I have written commentary and analysis; taught in a way I take to be progressive; helped to organise trade union activity; participated in campaigns against selective education or against the pressures of racism. Yet in the gaps between the analysis and the teaching and the campaigning have existed silences that I suspect represent a common difficulty on the left. What has been missing has been a response fully adequate to the ideological richness and political inventiveness of the right, and fully alert to the hesitations and the weak points in its programme. If this book contributes to the formation of such a response, and if the charter can lead to the drawing up of popular, plainly stated alternatives to a narrow, zealous and deeply inhumane policy, they will have been worth the effort of writing.

Bibliography

Chapter 1

An interpretation of Conservative policy that emphasizes its regressive aspects is Brian Simon's *Bending the Rules* (1988). An already classic analysis of British backwardness in education and in the economy is Correlli Barnett's *The Audit of War: the illusion and reality of Britain as a great nation* (1986). The achievements and the shortcomings of progressive reform have been much discussed. The account given here relies upon: Stephen J. Ball (ed.) *Comprehensive Schooling: a reader* (1984); D. Reynolds and M. Sullivan, with S. Murgatroyd, *The Comprehensive Experiment: A comparison of the selective and non-selective systems of school organisation* (1987); J. Westergaard and H. Resler, *Class in a Capitalist Society* (1976); Education Group, Centre for Contemporary Cultural Studies, *Unpopular Education: Schooling and Social Democracy since 1944* (1981); D. Hargreaves, *The Challenge for the Comprehensive School* (1982); K. Jones, *Beyond Progressive Education* (1983). Documents which demonstrate the evolution of reforming thought at an official level in the 1970s are the DES report, *Educational Priority*, Volume 1 (1972), the DES restricted-circulation paper, *School Education: Problems and Initiatives*, written for Prime Minister Callaghan in 1976, Callaghan's subsequent speech in October of that year at Ruskin College, which is extensively discussed in *Unpopular Education*, and in the Green Paper *Education in Schools: A Consultative Document*, published in 1977.

For a sense of the background to Conservative education policy, I have drawn from Andrew Gamble's two books, *Britain in Decline* (1981) and *The Free Economy and the Strong State* (1988), from William Keegan's *Mrs Thatcher's Economic Experiment* (1984), from Beatrix Campbell's *Iron Ladies* (1987), and from a number of detailed, perceptive articles in *New Left Review*, especially B. Jessop, K. Bonnett, S. Bromley, T. Ling, *Thatcherism and the Politics of Hegemony* (*NLR* 153 September/October 1985) and *Popular Capitalism, Flexible Accumulation and*

Left Strategy (*NLR* 165 September/October 1987); also Bill Schwarz's *Conservatism and Corporatism* (*NLR* 166 November/December 1987). Some of the tensions within Conservative educational politics are referred to in C. Chitty and D. Lawton, *The National Curriculum*, Bedford Way Papers 33 (1988), especially Clyde Chitty's article *Two Models of a National Curriculum*.

First-hand account of Conservative ideas and programmes can be found in the important, and very different, White Papers of 1972 and 1984–5, *Education: A Framework for Expansion*, and *Teaching Quality* and *Better Schools*; in the Conservative manifestos of 1979, 1983 and, especially, the two-part document of 1987: *Our First Eight Years and The Next Moves Forward*; in the Education Reform Act of 1988; and in the copious writings and speeches of Sir Keith Joseph and of Kenneth Baker – especially Joseph's speeches to the North of England Education Conference in January 1984 on the Curriculum, January 1985 on the 'management of the teaching force', and January 1986 on training policies, and his thoughts on History and on Geography (*The Times Educational Supplement* 17.2.84 and 21.6.84). Baker's contributions can be found particularly in his speech on the teaching of English (7.11.86 in Pangbourne, Berkshire), his address to the Church of England on religious matters (February 1989), and in the commentaries of his anthology, *The Faber Book of English History in Verse* (1988). The texts of speeches by Baker and by Joseph are contained in press releases from the DES.

The teachers' disputes of the 1970s and 1980s are chronicled in Roger V. Seifert, *Teacher Militancy: A History of Teacher Strikes 1896–1987* (1987), and discussed by Gerald Grace and by Richard Pietrasik in *Teachers: The Culture and Politics of Work*, ed. M. Lawn and G. Grace (1987).

Chapter 2

The first part of this chapter leans upon the discussions of the significance of '1968' by Anthony Barnett in *Soviet Freedom* (1988) and by Regis Debray, *A Modest Contribution to the Rites and Ceremonies of the Tenth Anniversary*, NLR 115, May/June 1979. The varieties of right-wing thinking are distinguished by

Gamble, in *The Free Economy and The Strong State*, and in the collection edited by Ruth Levitas, *The Ideology of the New Right* (1986), especially the article by David Edgar on *The Free and the Good*. The funding of the right's think tanks is investigated in *Labour Research*, October 1987.

The importance of the consumer in conservative thought is discussed in Hilary Wainwright's *Labour: A Tale of Two Parties* (1987). The role of the press in elaborating the characteristics of new right ideology is well described in Nancy Murray's *Anti-racists and other demons: the press and ideology in Thatcher's Britain (Race and Class* XXVII 3 1986). Examples of the press's work can be found in the *Mail on Sunday*'s coverage of Brent – 19.10.86 and 15.11.87. Tom Nairn's chapter, *English Nationalism: the case of Enoch Powell*, in *The Break-up of Britain* (new edition, 1981) is essential to understanding the right's thinking about culture, as is Gillian Seidel's *Culture, Nation and 'Race' in the British and French New Right*, published in the Levitas collection.

The chapter refers to numerous pamphlets, manifestos and articles by the new right. The Black Papers were published on five occasions between 1969 and 1977. The first three, edited by C.B. Cox and A.E. Dyson, are collected in *The Black Papers on Education – A revised edition* (1971). The fourth, *The Fight for Education*, was published in 1975. The fifth, *Black Paper 1977*, was edited by Cox and Rhodes Boyson. Boyson's own book, *The Crisis in Education* was published in 1975. The accuracy of the Black Papers' claims is assessed in Nigel Wright's *Progress in Education* (1977). Their political impact is discussed in *Unpopular Education* and in *Beyond Progressive Education*.

Discussion of Roger Scruton's contributions is for the most part based on the collection of articles he wrote for *The Times*, published in book form as *Untimely Tracts* (1987). To these should be added his article *The Myth of Cultural Relativism*, in Frank Palmer (ed.) *Anti-Racism: an Assault on Education and Value* (1987); his book *The Meaning of Conservatism* (1980), and the pamphlet, *Education and Indoctrination* that he produced in collaboration with D. O'Keefe and A. Ellis-Jones in 1985. Scruton also contributed to the Hillgate Group's pamphlet, *Whose Schools? A radical manifesto*, in 1986.

Ray Honeyford's most controversial article is *Education and*

BIBLIOGRAPHY

Race: an alternative view, published in the *Salisbury Review* of Winter 1984. Others which are discussed here are *The Right Education* from the *Salisbury Review* of January 1985, and *Anti-racist rhetoric*, which is printed in the Palmer collection. Articles about Honeyford include the Centre for Policy Studies pamphlet by A. Brown, *The Trials of Honeyford: problems in multi-cultural education* (1985), and *A Severed Head*, by Ian Jack, in *Before the oil ran out: Britain 1977–87* (1987).

The two free market contributions to educational debate that are quoted here are the pamphlet *No Turning Back*, issued under the names of ten MPs by the Conservative Political Centre in 1985, and the *Omega File* of the Adam Smith Institute, published as a whole in 1985, but compiled in the period 1983–4.

Marenbon's pamphlet, *English, Whose English* and Beattie's *History in Peril, May Parents Preserve It* were both published by the Centre for Policy Studies in 1987. They had been preceded by other right-wing statements about English and History teaching, including *English: Two decades of Attrition* by A. Barcan in the 1986 Social Affairs Unit collection *The Wayward Curriculum*, edited by D. O'Keefe; G. Partington's *History: Rewritten to Ideological Fashion* in the same volume; and Tom Hastie's *History, Race and Propaganda* in the collection edited by Palmer. Sheila Lawlor's *Correct Core: Simple Curricula for English, Maths and Science* (CPS 1988) makes an intervention from the right into debate about the content of the national curriculum.

The influence of the right's ideas on the attitudes and policies of Conservative politicians is frequently captured in their contribution to parliamentary debates. See, for instance, *Hansard* of 10.6.86 for debate on the 1986 Education Bill, 30.10.86 on Teachers' Pay, and 1.12.87 on the Education Reform Bill. Its impact on reformers can be measured, for instance, in Melanie Phillips' articles in *The Guardian*, such as those of 11.9.87 and 3.2.89. The Procrustean account of the national curriculum may be found in the DES consultative document on *The National Curriculum 5–16* (1987).

Finally, for an account of comparable developments in the education system of the USA, see Ira Shor's *Culture Wars: Society and Schooling in the Conservative Restoration* (1986), and for a general account of the American new right, Mike Davis, *Prisoners of the American Dream* (1986), especially Chapter 4, from which the Vigurie quotation is taken.

Chapter 3

The accounts of British industrial decline, and of the contribution that education and culture have made to it rely on Barnett, on Martin Wiener's *English Culture and the Decline of the Industrial Spirit*: 1850–1980 (1981), and on G. Roderick and M. Stephens' *The British Malaise: Industrial Performance, Education and Training in Britain Today* (1982), especially D. Aldcroft's article on *Britain's Economic Decline 1870–1980*. For the political weakness of industrial capital see G. Ingham, *Capitalism Divided* (London 1984) and C. Leys, *Thatcherism and Manufacturing: A Question of Hegemony* (*NLR* 151 May/June 1985).

The 'modernizing' critique of education can also be found: in C. Avent, *Laying the Foundations: Schools and Industry*, in the Roderick and Stephens collection; in the Institute of Manpower Studies, *Competence and Competition: Training in the Federal Republic of Germany, the United States and Japan*, written for the National Economic Development Council and for the MSC in 1984; in the articles edited by Digby Anderson for the Social Affairs Unit, *Trespassing: Businessmen's Views on the Education System* (1984); and, of course, by David Young, in *Knowing How and Knowing That: A Philosophy of the Vocational*, the Haldane Memorial lecture published by Birkbeck College, London in 1984. A less narrowly vocational view is taken in, for instance, *Education: Investment in Human Assets*, the Standing Conference on Schools' Science and Technology Annual Lecture (1984). This was given by Sir Dennis Rooke, Chairman of British Gas.

Progressive education is discussed, inter alia: in my own book, referred to earlier; in several contributions – especially that by Stuart Hall – in *Is there anyone here from education?* edited by J. Donald and A. Wolpe (London 1984); and in Valerie Walkerdine, *Developmental Psychology and child-centred pedagogy: the insertion of Piaget into early education*; in J. Henriques et al. *Changing the Subject: Psychology, social regulation and subjectivity* (1984). The quotation from John Watts, headteacher of Countesthorpe College, Leicestershire, is taken from *Schools on*

Trial: the trials of democratic comprehensives by C. Fletcher et al. (1985). The incorporation of aspects of the progressivism into the modernizing project can be traced: in C. Richards (staff inspector at the DES), *Primary Education in England: An analysis of some recent issues and developments* in S. Delamont, *The Primary School Teacher* (1987); in the article by Jamieson and Watts, *Squeezing out Enterprise, Times Educational Supplement* 18.12.87; in the HMI *Curriculum Matters* series, especially the 1984 pamphlet on English teaching; and, most plainly, in the collection edited by S. Ranson, B. Taylor and T. Brighouse, *The Revolution in Education and Training* 1986).

Initial stages in the development of the National Curriculum, which show something of the results of negotiation between the demands of Conservative policy, and the traditional thinking of what the right calls the educational establishment, are set out in: *The National Curriculum Task Group on Assessment and Testing: A Report* (the 'Black Report'); in the *Report of the Committee of Enquiry into the teaching of English Language* (the 'Kingman' report); and in the 'proposals of the Secretary of State for Education and Science and the Secretary of State for Wales' on *English for ages 5 to 11* (the 'Cox report'), on *Science for ages 5 to 16*, and on *Mathematics for ages 5 to 16*. All these documents were published in 1988 – which says something about the pace of change.

The growth and influence of the MSC has been the subject of several critiques. Most notable are Caroline Benn and John Fairley's 1986 collection, *Challenging the MSC: On Jobs, Education and Training*, which includes the excellent article by Andy Green, *The MSC and the three-tier structure of Further Education*; Dan Finn's *Training without Jobs: New Deals and Broken Promises* (1987); and Pat Ainley's *From School to YTS: Education and Training in England and Wales 1944–87* (1988). The educational impact of ideas generated or promoted by the MSC is charted in Phil Cohen's article, *Against the New Vocationalism*, in Bates et al., *Schooling for the Dole? A new vocationalism* (1984); in R. Dale (ed.) *Education, Training and Employment: towards a new vocationalism* (1985); and in *TVEI and Secondary Education: a critical appraisal*, ed. D. Gleeson (1987). In this latter volume, Gary McCulloch's article, *History and Policy: The Politics of TVEI*, is valuable. More positive accounts of TVEI can be found in R. Wallace, *Introducing Technical and Vocational Education* (1985) from which details of the Hertfordshire scheme are taken, in Maureen O'Connor's account in *The Guardian* (23.10.84), and in the Ranson/Taylor/ Brighouse collection, which, in R. Pryke's article, contains material on the Devon scheme. Valerie Hannon's critical article, *The new education: what's in it for girls?* – also found in the Ranson et al. collection is especially useful. The most enthusiastic account of education and the enterprise economy is the White Paper jointly produced by the Department of Employment and the DES in 1986 – *Working Together: Education and Training.*

The Greater London Council's attempts to develop a critique of the sort of approach outlined in the joint White Paper can be found in *The London Labour Plan* (1986) and *The London Industrial Strategy* (1985). They are supplemented by Peter Townsend, with Paul Corrigan and Uwe Kowarzik, *Poverty and Labour in London* (1987).

Chapter 4

Critiques of the effectiveness of MSC policy as an instrument of modernization can be found in: *Work for the Future: A New Strategy for Training and Employment*, published by the Society of Civil and Public Servants in 1986; and in *Education and Training: Options for Labour*, report of a Parliamentary Spokesman's study group, also 1986.

Baker's claims about the high-quality education of the future were reported in the *Times Educational Supplement* of 23.1.87. The account of the workforces of Silicon Valley is by R. Howard, *Second-class in Silicon Valley*, in *Working Papers for a New Society*, September/October 1981. The most up-to-date picture of the problems of teacher supply is given by the survey carried out by the Institute of Manpower Studies for the NUT, publicized by the union in January 1989. This is a response to the DES Consultative Paper of 1988, *Qualified Teacher Status*.

Dissident right-wing views on 'relevance' are contained in Olvier Letwin's CPS pamphlet on *The Aims of Schooling: the importance of grounding* (1987), and in Frank Palmer's contribution to *The Wayward Curriculum – English: Reducing learning to short-cut skills.*

199

Chapter 5

The views of Labour politicians have been gathered from the following articles and speeches:

Neil Fletcher: Speech to the Socialist Education Association, Brighton, 30.9.87; article in *TES* of 6.11.87;. article in *New Socialist*, December 1987; speech to a Fabian Society conference, *Beating the Blues*, London, December 1987, reported in *The Teacher*, 14.12.87.

Jack Straw: speech in debate on second reading of Education Bill, 1.12.87; remarks quoted by Martin Francis in *Race and Class XXIX 3*, Winter 1988.

Jack Cunningham: comments on Labour's attitude to the 1987 Local Government Bill (Clause 28), quoted in *The Guardian*, 9.12.87.

Giles Radice: article in *Socialism and Education* Vol. 12, Number 3, Autumn 1986; article in *TES* 17.5.85.

Neil Kinnock: article in *The Observer*, 30.3.86.

Bryan Gould: remarks on individuality quoted by Hilary Wainwright, in *Labour: A Tale of Two Parties*; further remarks in an article in *The Guardian*, 4.9.87.

James Callaghan: 'Ruskin' speech of October 1976, discussed in *Unpopular Education* and *Beyond Progressive Education*.

The overall thinking involved in Labour's Policy Review can be found in the initial policy review documents presented to party conference in September 1988, and also in issues of the Communist Party's *Marxism Today*, especially the issue of October 1988: *New Times – a Marxism Today special on Britain in the nineties*.

At the time of writing, the report of the 'Burnage Inquiry' has not been printed. Extracts from it can be found in the heavily cut version issued by Manchester City Council in 1988: *The Burnage Inquiry (Extract of Report for public use)*, and in the special supplement of the *Manchester Evening News*, 25.4.88. The DPRE is described in a document entitled *Development Programme for Race Equality*, issued by the London Borough of Brent in 1987. The critical assessment of the relationship between teachers' strikes and radical educational issues is made by Gus John in *The Black Working Class Movement in Education and*

Schooling and the 1985/6 Teachers' Dispute, issued by the Black Parents' Movement in 1986.

Chapter 6

The predictions concerning future conflict over the national curriculum are those of Helen Simons, *Teacher Professionalism and the National Curriculum,* in D. Lawton and C. Chitty (ed.), *The National Curriculum,* Bedford Way Papers 33 (1988). Hugh Lauder's article is *Traditions of Socialism and Education Policy,* edited by P. Brown and H. Lauder (1988).

Discussions of the early Soviet experience of education can be found in S. Castles and W. Wustenberg, *The Education of the Future* (1979). Dewey's ideas are authoritatively set out in *Democracy and Education* (1921). My account of Gramsci's ideas is based on: *Selections from the Prison Notebooks,* especially the sections *The Intellectuals* and *On Education* and the notes on *The Study of Philosophy,* edited by Q. Hoare and G. Nowell-Smith (1971); *Selections from Cultural Writings,* edited by D. Forgacs and G. Nowell-Smith (1985) and *Letters from Prison* (ed. L. Lawner, 1979). Harold Entwistle's interpretation of Gramsci is *Antonio Gramsci: Conservative Schooling for Radical Politics* (1979). Maureen Stone's book is *The Education of the Black Child in Britain: the myth of multi-racial education* (1981).

Books and articles which explore the relationship between personal experience, historical–sociological exploration and intellectual development include: H. Giroux, *Theory and Resistance in Education: A Pedagogy for the Opposition (1983) Critical Pedagogy and Cultural Power,* ed. D. Livingstone (1987) – especially the article by D. Ashenden et al. on *Teachers and Working-class Schooling;* D. Bertaux (ed.) *Biography and Society: The Life-history approach to the Social Sciences* (1981); C. Ginzburg, *The Cheese and the Worms* (1980); T. Pateman, *Language, Truth and Politics* (1980); J. Williamson, *Is there anyone here from a Classroom?, Screen* 26.1 January 1985; *English Teaching and Class – A discussion document,* by Hilda Kean, ILEA 1988; Richard Hatcher, *Anti-racist learning: a local studies approach* in *Multi-cultural teaching* Winter 7.1 1988. The reference to nineteenth-century ruling-class attitudes is taken from D. Thompson *Popular Politics in the Industrial Revolution* (1984).

Finally, the 'Charter' is a draft written by me for a document submitted by the Socialist Teachers Alliance to the Chesterfield Socialist Conference in 1988. A final version, slightly amended, is now being publicized by the STA, as an attempt to popularize an educational programme that is less in awe of the Conservative achievement than those currently fashionable on the left. I have let the document stand as it was originally written, rather than amend sections which have since (already!) become outdated by events – the references, for instance, to the MSC and to the all-embracing nature of the national curriculum.

Index

CRITICAL ACCLAIM FOR CRITICAL BOOKS

The Enchanted Glass: Britain and its Monarchy

Tom Nairn

£8.95 paperback   ISBN 0 09 172955 6

. . . a long and brilliant meditation on the nature of the British state, its identity and national culture . . . For Nairn is a republican in a way that many, even on the left, have forgotten to be.

R.W. Johnson, *London Review of Books*

. . . (a) dazzling, cliché-nailing essay . . . This was a book crying out to be written.

Ben Pimlott, *Observer*

The power of Tom Nairn's book lies in its unsparing depiction of Britain as a cultural sarcophagus, packed with fossilised attitudes.

Neil Berry, *The Guardian*

Nairn is very good on the Investiture. He is very good on many things, from the royal doll's house to the Poets Laureate . . . His tone is a mixture of amusement and suppressed fury at the fact that people who disapprove of the monarchy still claim that it is nevertheless essentially 'unimportant'.

Francis Wheen, *Literary Review*

Nairn goes about his task of 'quiet Republicanism' with panache and good humour.

Blitz

The Enchanted Glass . . . is an enormously important book, a rare and intelligent republican glimmer.

The Listener

Games with Shadows

Neal Ascherson

£7.95   ISBN 0 09 173018 X

The man who should be reading *Games with Shadows* is Neil
Kinnock . . . the essays map out plausible ground for a socialist
alternative capable of being something more than a complaint
against Thatcher . . .

Bruce Page, *The Spectator*

He ranges freely back through the twentieth century to the
sixteenth, and back again to the lost world of the Picts and the
Druids . . . His idiosyncratic intelligence and shameless erudition
give me hope . . .

Michael Frayn, *The Observer*

He is . . . scholarly, witty, cosmopolitan, radical, iconoclastic and
sometimes emotionally compelling . . . Ascherson is the best
British political columnist (and) among the best in Europe.

Stephen Howe, *New Statesman*

He writes beautifully, with an ease and vividness and grace that
are enormously attractive.

John Dunn, *The Times Literary Supplement*

A polymath and polyglot with a fluent and mordant style . . .
an astringent antidote to the wave of 'Glorious Revolution'
emollience . . .

Christopher Hitchens, *Literary Review*

Ascherson towers above his peers in his consistent seriousness of
purpose, his style and his political engagement.

Paul Anderson, *Tribune*

Trading Places: The Future of the European Community

John Palmer

£6.95   ISBN 0 09 173187 9

A short but challenging book . . . concerned about the EC's place
in the world and how it may evolve. John Palmer is that rare bird
– a left wing socialist who has consistently championed European
integration.

Dick Leonard, *Sunday Times*

The Gorbachev Phenomenon: A Historical Interpretation

Moshe Lewin

An outstanding interpretation by an outstanding historian of
Soviet society . . . well-informed and exceptionally apt.

Teodor Shanin

A timely book

Anthony Barnett, author of *Soviet Freedom*

This book does not deal with Gorbachev as a person or politician.
It analyses the social and political forces that have produced him.

Liverpool Daily Post

A brief review cannot do justice to so sparkling an essay. This slim
volume, based on a lifetime's scholarly research into social change
since the revolution, is compulsory summer reading for anyone
who would or should understand the Gorbachev phenomenon.

Edward Acton, *Observer*